JUMP
SHOOTING
TO A HIGHER
DEGREE

JUMP SHOOTING TO A HIGHER DEGREE

My Basketball Odyssey

....

SHELDON ANDERSON

University of Nebraska Press

LINCOLN

Library of Congress Cataloging-in-Publication Data
Names: Anderson, Sheldon R., 1951– author.
Title: Jump shooting to a higher degree: my basketball
odyssey / Sheldon Anderson.
Description: Lincoln: University of Nebraska Press, 2021.
Identifiers: LCCN 2020056568
ISBN 9781496226488 (paperback)
ISBN 9781496228697 (epub)
ISBN 9781496228703 (pdf)
Subjects: LCSH: Anderson, Sheldon R., 1951– | Basketball
players—United States—Biography. | College teachers—
United States—Biography.
Classification: LCC GV884.A555 A3 2021
DDC 796.323092 [B]—dc23
LC record available at https://lccn.loc.gov/2020056568

Set in Questa by Laura Buis.

CONTENTS

ILLUSTRATIONS

ACKNOWLEDGMENTS

"Acknowledgments" seem redundant in a memoir that is an homage to the many people, from Moorhead, Minnesota, to Warsaw, Poland, who have enriched my life on and off the playing field. I would like to give a special thanks to Ohioans Marilyn Elzey, Jeff Kimball, and Linda Musmeci for their enduring support and friendship. Marilyn read the manuscript and corrected my many grammatical errors. I would also like to thank Dave Smith, with whom I have often discussed the process of writing history.

In addition, I am indebted to Rob Taylor and the talented team at the University of Nebraska Press, who made the process of publishing this book seamless.

Last but not least, I would like to acknowledge my brother, Randy, without whom this sports story would not have been possible. Thanks, bro.

JUMP
SHOOTING
TO A HIGHER
DEGREE

Prologue

I am frequently asked if I am a basketball player, and I always say no.... Basketball is what I do, it's not who I am.

—BILL RUSSELL

Six-year-olds do dumb things. For some reason young Sheldon decided to sprint across Moorhead's busy Third Avenue South and ran smack dab into the side of an old Packard. The driver leapt out of the car to see if I was okay, but other than my surprise at hitting a car of all things—in the middle of a street—I got up off the pavement and told him I was fine. If I had begun my mad dash two seconds earlier there would be no basketball story to tell here. The Christian God was a big part of my life in those days, but I don't credit him with holding my start back a tick. That kid got some mighty dumb luck, and he's had it ever since.

Writing a memoir is a hubristic endeavor. In my case, why would anyone want to read a story about a northern Minnesota kid falling in love with his basketball in the 1950s, a professional cager in West Germany in the 1970s, or a PhD candidate lacing up his sneakers in communist Poland? Is my story unique, enlightening, or at all interesting?

Two years before the fall of the communist regime in Poland and the collapse of the Warsaw Pact in 1989, a small sports club in Lublin offered me room and board to play basketball. Without any other way to get into Poland to finish my dissertation research, I took it. I am sure that I am the only American scholar to fund his dissertation research by playing semi-professional basketball in a communist country. Researching by day and playing by night, I traveled throughout the country with the team. I was the only American player in the league at the time—an eyewitness to the dire conditions in Poland shortly before the collapse of communism and the fall of the Iron Curtain.

This book is not a recounting of the games—the wins, the losses, or the points I scored—but rather a commentary on the people I met, the places where I played, and those historic times. In over six decades of playing basketball, I have teamed up with many interesting and diverse characters, from childhood friends in Moorhead to high school and college teammates in inner-city Minneapolis, from Ivory Tower eggheads to Germans and Poles.

There are even some brushes with greatness in the story and, in some cases, brushes with ignominy. I sat at a dinner next to Muhammad Ali, played ball against NBA Hall of Famers Kevin McHale and Oscar Robertson, house-sat for Vice President Walter Mondale during his run for the presidency in 1984, and practiced at the Munich gym where the Soviets beat the United States in the infamous, controversial 1972 Olympic gold medal basketball game.

Some of the people I write about at length have nothing to do with basketball, such as my friends in the former East Germany and Poland. Liselore Detzer from Magdeburg was my mother's age. Detzer experienced a catastrophic twentieth-century history, having lived through the Depression, the Third Reich, and the destruction of her city in World War II. After U.S. troops retreated from Magdeburg into their western occupation zone in 1945, the Soviet Red Army arrived to install a communist East German regime for the next forty years of her life. Macek and Basia Roszkowski generously took me into their cramped Warsaw apartment in 1987, along with their four children and several sailmakers who came in to sew every day.

There is, I think, something in this memoir for sports fans, who will enjoy the reflections on the sociology of basketball, the world's second most popular game. Historians will be interested in my observations about life behind the Iron Curtain in the last stages of the Cold War. Midwesterners will savor the local flavor, and academics will resonate with stories from the rarefied air of higher education.

As a professional historian, I have always envied novelists, journalists, and film documentarians who do not have to bother with those pesky footnotes that provide evidence of the truth of their stories. One of my favorite college English professors once told a newspaper reporter, "I enjoyed all sorts of fine students at Augsburg [College], such as Sheldon Anderson, the president's son, who became a professional basketball star in Italy and later coached the Polish national team." I never played in Italy or coached the Polish national team, but it made for good copy, I guess.

I have always thought it odd that historians put autobiographies in the category of primary sources, as though their veracity is unquestioned. Memories are flawed, political agendas seep into the narrative, and embarrassing moments are glossed over or completely omitted. I am guilty on the last charge, but I have no political motives here. My intention is for the reader to look at my friends more than look at me. I am just a fellow traveler along this serpentine road who would have gotten nowhere without the many friends who picked me up along the way. They are my great fortune and inspiration for this memoir.

For that reason, rather than including photos of the places mentioned in this chronicle (which can be found on the internet), I share photos of my friends and family. Although the resolution often is lacking, they are priceless images that are sharply etched in my memory.

Many of the names in the book have been changed to protect the guilty.

1

Of God and Games

G rowing up in the 1950s on the Red River of the North in the small town of Moorhead, Minnesota, my prospects of becoming a cowboy seemed better than playing pro basketball. The romance of the old West was a powerful elixir for a kid living on the fringes of the Dakota prairie. I wanted to ride horses like the cowpokes in Edna Walker Chandler's *Cowboy Sam* children's books, twirl a rifle like Chuck Connor on TV's *The Rifleman*, quick-draw like Steve McQueen on *Wanted, Dead or Alive*, and sleep out under the stars like Ward Bond on *Wagon Train*.

There weren't many basketball games on TV in the 1950s, but a lot of primetime westerns. They all had catchy theme songs, like "Paladin, Paladin, where do you roam . . . Paladin, Paladin, far, far from home." Paladin stood out as the coolest hombre in the West—a man's man. Actor Richard Boone wore black head to toe and had a dazzling silver chess knight on his holster. My favorite Christmas gift was a Paladin cowboy outfit. I have never fired a real gun, but with exploding caps the Paladin six-shooter sounded genuine enough. Paladin's calling card, which was included in my kit, simply read, "Wire Paladin, San Francisco." I thought "Wire" was his first name.

I used to imagine myself on the dusty trail far, far from home, and tried to sleep under my cowboy hat on the bedroom floor. After a few minutes on the imaginary dirt I always slunk back to my comfy bed, a defeated city slicker. I even got a Red Ryder BB gun like Ralphie in the holiday classic

A Christmas Story. I didn't shoot my eye out, but I lost my desire to fire it after a lucky shot dropped an innocent little bird minding its own business. I was a killer—there was no western romance about that.

My dad, Oscar, was the head pastor at Trinity Lutheran Church in Moorhead. He often told the story about the time I left my toy guns on the altar as parishioners showed up for Sunday services. Sadly, today churchgoers would head for the hills at the sight.

I had no relatives on the range, so cowboying was out. Playing sports in Moorhead wasn't easy either, but at least you didn't need a horse. The long winter is deadly cold in the fertile, flat Red River Valley where there is nothing to stop the incessant, howling west wind. "Oh yah," people up there really *do* talk like police officer Marge Gunderson in the movie *Fargo*. We had pet cats in those days. When a couple of them got caught outside in the subzero cold they snuggled onto the warmth of the engine of Dad's baby-blue and white Chrysler DeSoto. What a horrible sound it was when he started the car and the cats got hacked up by the cooling fan. They had to be put down. "Oh geez," Marge would have said sadly.

The grim history of farm life at the turn of the century in that godforsaken region is chillingly captured in John Hanson's Cannes Film Festival prizewinner *Northern Lights*. The haunting *shhh* of the cold wind underscores the soundtrack. It took a hardy type to make it there, as the main character in the movie observes: "If we work we live, if we don't we die." The long winter tested the sanity of the immigrant farmers. In Ole Rolvaag's novel *Giants in the Earth*, Per Hansa realized that he had to get his sons out of the house, regardless of the cold outside: "They went outside and attacked the wood pile. They sawed and they chopped. . . . This work cheered them up and kept their minds occupied, though the winter was bitterly cold and inclement. They toiled at it from early morning until late at night. . . . The woodpile lasted exactly four days; when they had chopped up the last stick there was nothing left for them to do outside. Then they sat idle again. The bad spell of weather held out interminably." It is no wonder that North Dakota is the only U.S. state that had fewer residents in 2000 than it had a century before.

My older brother, Randy, thankfully ushered me into the world of ball games. Before we moved from Minneapolis to Moorhead when I was three, Randy got interested in sports by going with Dad to Minneapolis Millers Minor League baseball games and Minneapolis Lakers NBA basketball games. Los Angeles should never have been able to steal our team *and* our nickname. Show me a lake in Los Angeles and I'll show you a palm tree in Minneapolis. Randy calls them the Los Angeles Reservoirs. New Orleans losing the Jazz was even worse. The Utah Jazz. Uff da.

Dad was a good swimmer, but with ten thousand lakes, Minnesotans *had* to be. Ball games were not Oscar's forte. I don't think he ever played a game of catch with me. One time "The Big O," as Randy and I used to call all 5'6" of him, took me out to the driveway to show me the two-handed set shot. He hadn't channeled the real Big O—NBA Hall of Famer Oscar Robertson. Dad's anachronistic tutorial was kind of like the telegraph I had to make in junior high shop class. Neither was exactly cutting edge, but I guess I could have used the telegraph to wire Paladin.

Randy and I had no access to a gym, so we played hoops on the driveway of the parsonage. My dad's assistant pastor, Del Jacobson, helped us nail a backboard on the attached garage. Del was 6'3" and fancied himself as a pretty good ballplayer. He used to challenge Randy to play one-on-one, but if Randy beat him, Del went ballistic, like the abusive father Robert Duvall played in *The Great Santini*. One time Del threw a punch at Randy. "He's a red head," Mom explained, "and they're hot tempered." Today that carrot top might have faced an assault charge.

The house and garage were painted white, so when it rained or snowed, or if the ball inadvertently hit the water faucet on the house and flooded the court, the ball got dirty and left numerous pebbled stains on the walls, which were impossible to wash out. When it was below freezing, the court was more conducive to ice hockey. Oddly enough, only a few in town played that game in those days. Hockey was an Iron Range, Twin City, and Canadian-border sport.

From December to February it was impossible to play basketball outside. I invented nerf basketball, but the Andersons had no entrepreneurial instincts and never marketed it. I made a little hoop out of a coat hanger, laboriously tied together a string net, sawed a backboard out of plywood, and tacked it up in the parsonage basement. A tennis ball was the perfect size for the game. Eventually I made another basket on the opposite end of the basement so I could play full court. Imagining that I was one of my favorite NBA players, I could do a fancy array of dunks on the six-foot hoop. For some reason Randy didn't join me down there much, although he says he did.

I fell in love with basketball, a game like no other. Maybe it is the allure of the silky tickle of the twine, the symmetrical splash of the net. It is a beautiful sight to behold. Anytime I see a perfectly hung net, it beckons for the onomatopoetic swish.

The basketball is a unique game piece. No other sport turns *ball* into another noun for a player (*baller*), and also into a verb, as in, "You ballin'?" No one says, "Let's go tennisballin' or footballin'." Dedicated young ballers dribble their pill down the street and caress it in bed at night, working on their shot release. Soccer players might have a love affair with their ball, but do they hug it with their feet? Pitchers develop a special relationship with the seams on the baseball, but hitters want to knock the cover off of it, and a hard comebacker can cause serious injury. Baseball is one of the few sports in which runs are scored by the team without possession of the ball.

More than any other ball game, there is a direct correlation between basketball players' political and religious beliefs and style of play. Basketball players have a choice to be self-ish or giving. Soccer and football players *have to* pass the ball, but in basketball, if one player dominates the ball, the game becomes undemocratic and un-Christian. Didn't Jesus say, "It is more blessed to give than receive?" And it was Saint Luke who inspired the "give and go": "Give, and it will be given to you." Selfish basketball is also losing basketball; coaches often have to implore their players to "share" the ball. Only basketball uses *team* as an adjective to describe a desired style of play. Coaches don't implore their minions to play *team* football or *team* baseball.

My first basketball was a cheap plastic Voit, the Chevy of basketballs; you can still get one for under ten bucks on Amazon. The Voit barely bounced in the best of conditions. It really *was* a "rock," as Black guys started calling a basketball in the 1980s. Given that a winter crossover dribble was impossible, the Voit *had* to be shared. Lakers great Magic Johnson once said, "When you come down and create a shot for your teammate and they score off that creation, that's a beautiful feeling. To me, that's basketball."

Johnson knew how to play winning team basketball. When asked why he usually gave up the ball on the fast break, he gave this simple reply: "They won't run with me again if I don't." Despite the trend toward playing one-on-one in the NBA, the league champion has almost always shared the ball. Even Michael Jordan and LeBron James were great passers, relying on their teammates to hit big shots at crunch time. In this era of "one-and-dones" and rampant free-agent moves from team to team, it is hard to develop loyalty to any group of college or pro players, even if the laundry they wear has the hometown logo. I just root for teams that play the right way.

As a sexagenarian, I know that my workout future is in the swimming pool, but there is no camaraderie there. The team element of basketball keeps me playing to this day. In college, we had a signal for the "back door" cut to the basket for a layup. I used the same sign when I played in Germany and Poland. Years later in games with fellow academic Chris Elzey, who played in Poland as well, we used to yell, "Do tyl" in Polish, which loosely translates as "to the door." I am the only guy in a pickup game who still whispers for a teammate to go back door. It usually works, and makes both the passer and the scorer feel real good. Whenever we win a game on that play, I shout out Magic's line, "That's basketball!"

The sports seasons organized my childhood. Randy and I played and watched football in the fall, basketball in the winter, and baseball in the summer. Each sport brought the return of our heroes and a new season of hope, a new drama with familiar actors, a new plotline, and an unpredictable final act. That's why sports are the world's most popular cultural form. Everyone knows that Hamlet dies at the end of the play, but no one knows if a Yankee will hit the game-winning home run or a Celtic will nail the last-second shot. And if the game is tied at the end, you get an overtime, or maybe two or three. Bonus sports!

We played football and baseball on the lawn between the parsonage and the church. Randy was always the quarterback, which epitomized our relationship. I had to follow his play calls, or suffer a painful hammerlock or, worse, get pinned down on my back. I went hysterical in that position, much to his delight. I think I got that phobia from seeing kids lying flat on their back in a huge iron lung to save them from polio, the scourge of our generation. To this day I can't sleep on my back. I have to close my eyes and take a lot of deep breaths when I get an abdominal MRI.

Randy used to give me a penny to ride my bike down to the corner store to buy him ten cents' worth of candy. The grumpy old proprietor behind the glass candy case would stare down at me and growl, "Whaddayougonnahave?" Randy and I still mimic that old coot. I had Randy's shopping list, but my choices were tough. Dad gave me a dime in weekly allowance. There were a lot of good "penny candies" in those days, from red, green, and brown licorice rope twists to Black

Jacks—a combo black, pink, and white taffy. A box of cylindrical Snaps licorice pieces was two cents, but you had to be wary of the pink one that had a soapy aftertaste. A Snickers bar was a nickel, as was the larger Three Musketeers bar. What a deal that was.

Randy didn't want to take little brother to ball games with his buddies, but Mom made him. Left alone to take care of her four kids, she wanted the two boys out of her hair. But he taught me how to throw a football, to shoot a jumper, and not to bat cross-handed. We are in our seventies now, and communicate daily about the latest sports news. Randy still orders me around and big brother always knows best. As he likes to say when one of my many personal foibles repeatedly bug him—borrowing a line from Mr. Swiveller in Charles Dickens's *The Old Curiosity Shop*—"'Twas ever thus." Nonetheless I am forever indebted to him for being my sports dad.

I ran buttonhooks, down-and-outs, and long post patterns around the fir tree on the church side of the field. The birch on the left side had too many branches and leaves for Randy to thread a pass through there. During baseball season we burned patches in the grass at home, first, second, and third. Dad was not happy about the broken church windows, the basketball stains on the parsonage, and the bare spots on God's green grass, but Mom defended us. It was her little protest against the bourgeois strictures of life as a minister's wife.

The desecrated church grounds didn't bother my buddy Art Grandskov either. The grizzled old Trinity janitor used to buy me a soda pop and let me watch him feed coal into the massive church boiler. I imagined that the huge fire in the hole was what Hell was like, and I thought of the Old Testament story of Shadrach, Meshach, and Abenego (or "To-bed-we-go" as we used to joke). Babylonian king Nebuchadnezzar threw them into a fiery furnace for refusing to worship a false god. I was a craven little Goody Two-shoes in part because I didn't want to end up in that scary boiler.

1. Randy staged this shot of him pitching and me hitting, so the 1956 DeSoto was not really a backstop. Was I trying to emulate the White Sox's Nellie Fox? Is Randy doing his impression of the Giants' Juan Marichal? Trinity Lutheran Church is in the background, and the church grounds that we tore up playing football and baseball. Courtesy of the author.

I did commit two big sins. I thought I was surely headed to Hades when I took a nickel that was to go into the church collection plate and used it to buy an ink pen. "Thou shalt not steal," so when Dad found out I got the belt on my lyin' little ass. I only suffered that punishment one other time for rank disobedience, a breach of the fourth commandment to "honor thy father and mother." A short whipping was normal punishment in those days, and I'm no worse for it.

Randy and I were not the only ones who tore up the church grounds. I was one of the singers in Trinity Lutheran's Bach Boys' Choir. We always got in a game of catch before heading to practice under the stern eye of Trinity's choir director, Randolph "Casey" Jones. He told the *Fargo Forum* that he had formed the choir because "there is a tremendous difference in the singing abilities of boys. . . . Bach provided the challenge. The ranges and intricacies of his works are more easily executed by boys' voices than by ladies' voices." Who knew? Thank God we were born in the twentieth century and not in old Italy, where we might have been rendered high-pitched for the rest of our lives.

Jones's successor at Trinity Lutheran was Gay Fagerlund, which at the time was an ordinary Norwegian name. No joke. The poor guy would have to change his name today. Linguistic evolution has relegated old meanings to the dustbin of history. At Christmas we donned our gay apparel. People smoked fags. A queer person was just odd, and Dick, Woody, and Johnson were people's names. Casey Jones's daughter Becky married a guy named Beaver. Years later I innocently told my students that during some battle a general had "put his finger in the dike" to plug a breach in the front. The class snickered. Political correctness and new meanings of innocent words like *bush* and *wood*, which used to refer to flora, have teachers tiptoeing through a semantic minefield.

The Bach boys were pretty good, but we were really a novelty act. We got an invitation to sing at the "Christian Witness Pavilion" at the 1962 Seattle World's Fair as part of the "American Lutheran Church Week." According to the program, "This outstanding boys' choir is the only one of its kind in America and is being brought out especially for this week." We took along our baseball gloves and had plenty of down time to play a game. The *Seattle Times* announced, "Boys Choir Arrives, Ready for Bach or Ball." I was one of three boys featured in a photo that showed us holding a bat to decide who would hit first. Steve Johnk pulled "eagle claws" to get first ups. We weren't very baseball savvy in those days. The home field advantage is to get last ups, but we all wanted to hit first. That was more fun, and moms might have called us home to dinner in midinning.

Sports equipment was a precious commodity in those days. A parson's salary was meager. Although Dad got the preacher's discount at some businesses around Moorhead, he didn't get that deal at the sporting goods store. Randy and I nailed and taped together broken wooden bats and used shoelaces to repair broken mitts. We religiously oiled up our gloves with Vaseline, and tied a ball into it to form the pocket. When the pocket wore thin, we would put a damp sponge between the leather and the palm of the hand. Spitting into your glove and rubbing it in became an on-field ritual to keep the leather loose. We loved our mitts, which had a stamped autograph of one of our favorite players. The Louisville Sluggers had different models, too, from the thick-handled Jackie Robinson and Nellie Fox to the thin-handled Rocky Colavito (probably the coolest baseball name ever).

The Knothole Gang is a century-old tradition to get kids into baseball games for a pittance; some Minor League teams still have them. On Knothole Day Randy and I went to Minor League Fargo-Moorhead Twins baseball games at old Barnett Field in Fargo. Future Major Leaguers Jim "Mudcat" Grant played with the Twins, as did North Dakota native Roger Maris, who broke Babe Ruth's single-season home-run record in 1961. That record should still stand; the home run totals of the three "juicers" who hit more around the turn of the century shouldn't count.

When we moved back to Minneapolis in 1963, on Knothole Days I went to Minnesota Twins games at Metropolitan Stadium, arriving early for batting practice to catch blasts off the bat of the likes of Hall of Fame slugger Harmon Killebrew and Cuban great Tony Oliva. I never thought of getting their autograph on the ball and putting it on a shelf or selling it.

Bringing a baseball to the pickup game was a gift to the other players. The Anderson brothers brought most of the balls. The foul balls we caught at Twins games went right into play in our sandlot games at Moorhead High School or James H. Sharp Elementary School. Our game of three or four players on each side was called "pitcher's hand"—consisting maybe of a pitcher, a shortstop, and a left fielder. The hitting team provided the catcher, who stood ten feet behind the batter. We couldn't afford catcher's gear anyway. The hitter was out on a grounder if the fielder threw the ball to the pitcher before the batter made it to first base. We had a lot of rhubarbs about out calls at first (the mound), a great baseball tradition long gone in the age of incessant replay reviews and "going to the monitor."

The Moorhead High and Sharp School fields were not conducive to baseball. The grass rectangle behind the high school was a football field; hitting to right field was verboten because Eighth Street was about thirty feet beyond the infield. Sharp's playground consisted of loose pebbles, which ravished the smooth cover of a baseball into a shaggy mess, and wreaked havoc on the red stitches. When the cover came off we would use the inside of the ball. The pitcher didn't have to worry about a hard comebacker because the pebbles ate up any sharply hit ground ball.

The fields Randy and I played on and the big-league players we emulated ruined our baseball swings. We learned some horrible hitting habits, because you had to pull the ball. Without enough fielders, a hit to the right of center was a foul ball. And it was also considered wimpy, because you weren't quick enough to get around on the fastball. There was no fence at the Moorhead High field, so a liner to left rolled for a home run. Sharp's playground had a chain-link fence in left and the Bratlies' house behind it. We broke a lot of their windows, which put a fiscal damper on the round-tripper. I was a banjo hitter, so I never had the joy of seeing one go over the fence. Randy tried to emulate Mickey Mantle and pulled everything. In high school he had trouble hitting the deuce on the outside corner.

You won't see six or seven kids playing sandlot baseball anymore. Youth baseball is highly organized today. Kids have good coaches, batting cages, and plenty of fielders during batting practice. Hitting to the opposite field—going "oppo"—is good hitting, not effeminate.

Randy *did* play in an organized league in Moorhead and got on the most coveted Babe Ruth League team "Dairy Queen"—coveted not because the team was that good but because after every game the players got a Dilly Bar. As legend has it, the Moorhead Dairy Queen invented that ice-cream-on-a-stick treat, with chocolate, cherry, mint, and butterscotch varieties. Some of the sticks were stamped with "Free Dilly Bar." What a bonus. What a team!

Randy and I aped our heroes—switch-hitting Mantle's mighty cuts, Vic Power's pendulum warm-up swings, Harmon Killebrew's muscle-bound swats, or Nellie Fox's crouch. We tried to throw a knuckleball like Hoyt Wilhelm, sidearm like Don Drysdale, or tap the rubber twice like Mudcat Grant's windup. This was a time before coaches taught the same hitting and pitching styles, limiting extraneous movement before a swing or pitch. Gone are those quirky tics, like Cincinnati Reds great Joe Morgan's flapping elbow, or Los Angeles Dodgers pitcher Fernando Valenzuela "breathing through his eyelids like a lava lizard from the Galapagos," as Annie Savoy (Susan Sarandon) in *Bull Durham* put it.

Our favorite big-league heroes were like family. There was no ubiquitous media to air players' dirty laundry; beat writers adhered to a code of secrecy about players' private lives. Unless they got into some barroom brawl, we rarely heard about the drunken escapades of Yankees Mantle, Whitey Ford, and Billy Martin. The dalliances of Wilt Chamberlain, Paul Hornung, or Joe Namath didn't make the dailies either. Women's sports, except for the quadrennial Olympics and an occasional tennis or golf tournament, barely made the newspapers.

In the early 1960s there were only sixteen Major League Baseball teams, fourteen NFL teams, and nine NBA teams. There was no free agency in those days and many star players played their whole career with one team, creating a bond between the players and fans. Many players had to find jobs in the off-season to make ends meet. The system was patently unfair to the players, but they were just like us. We loved our boys and booed the enemy. The Dodgers hated the Giants, the Cardinals hated the Cubs, and the Red Sox hated the Yankees. One wonders if a team that showed loyalty to their best players today would draw hometown fans even if their team didn't always win.

Sports was our passion and the balls were our deities, but Randy and I got chiseled out of hundreds of hours of valuable playing time by church services, obligatory devotions after every supper, and the old canard that if you swim within one hour after eating you would get cramps and drown. We spent much of the summer at our cabin on Bad Medicine Lake in northern Minnesota near the headwaters of the mighty Mississippi, which trickles out of Lake Itasca. I have calculated that I lost at least a thousand hours of water time because of that fallacious rule.

But then pain always came before pleasure in the pious Anderson household. Lutherans believe that only the grace of God gets you to heaven, but living a chaste life helped, I guess. Prior to opening gifts on Christmas Eve, my elder sister Donna, Randy, and I had to write and perform a Christmas pageant (caboose baby Gracia got out of it after Dad left the ministry). We chose the hymns and the Bible readings, and decided on the roles we would play in Bethlehem. We had to make a program just like the one at a church service. We used Elmer's glue and glitter to sparkle it up. I tried to rush through the whole affair so I could open up my three or four gifts. Grandma Anderson's was always Old Spice soap-on-rope. Whoopee! On Christmas morning we emptied our stockings, which were filled with things that Santa had brought overnight—an assortment of nuts, an orange, and the big prize, a book of Life Savers hard candies. I'm sure that the nuts and oranges were what the folks got in their stockings during the Depression. They were nothing special to us ingrates.

Sundays really tested our patience. Even at the lake we drove twenty miles to church services in Ponsford, Minnesota. Dad was a gifted and passionate orator who really got worked up in the pulpit. I was three years old when he got particularly loud during one sermon, prompting me to shout out from the pew, "Dad, why are you yelling?" That got a good laugh from the parishioners, too.

Dad didn't think much of Ponsford's itinerant minister's homiletics, but we went anyway, not because Dad wanted to make sure we got to heaven, but because he did not want it to be known that he was skipping church. Or maybe it was just habit. Aside from the musty old church, my memory of that town is the stark poverty of the Ojibwe Indians living in dilapidated, dirt-floor houses. I remember the folks commenting on the TV antennae on every shack, as if the Indians did not have their priorities straight.

Dad was such a good preacher that the other Lutherans on the lake asked him to conduct a Sunday morning service so they didn't have to make the drive to Ponsford. The congregation gathered in our cabin for the service and the following potluck of divine Lutheran baked goods and crappy Folgers coffee. The music at those services was really good. Paul J. Christensen, the well-known conductor of the Concordia (Moorhead) College Choir, lived on the lake, as did Casey Jones, Dad's choir director at Trinity Lutheran. Jones leased an island from the Indians who by some old treaty still owned it. Lutherans can really belt out an inspiring rendition of "A Might Fortress Is Our God." The gathering got so big that there was no room to park the boats, so the local resort owner built a loft for the service, where "The Chapel of the Good Creation" is held to this day.

During baseball season Randy and I raced to read the baseball box scores in the morning *Fargo Forum*. There were some 150 of those mornings in the summer (given doubleheaders). I loved the simple four columns that showed the at-bats, runs, hits, and runs batted in. Fours in the first and third slots were pure symmetry—representing a perfect day at the plate. I only had one of those in my high school career; my son, O Maxwell (the O stands for Oscar), got one in high school, too. I printed out his box score—4 4 4 5—and framed it. It looked *so* good, but alas, O Max was indifferent.

For decades after World War II, the Sunday *Forum* featured a beautiful, peach-colored sports section, which Dad hid from Randy and me because he didn't want us to be late for Sunday School, church services, and the interminable meal that followed. The Sunday menu was always pork chops, baked chicken, or roast beef, potatoes, and carrots, peas, or green beans. Mom was not a good cook. In fact she hated most of the obligations of a housewife and parson's spouse. We grew up in the era of frozen food, and she made the most of it. We had a diverse cuisine including fish sticks, tater tots, and ethnic foods like Chef Boyardee hamburger pizzas and canned La Choy chow mein. Canned asparagus had a very peculiar odor and taste. But what a treat it was to get to eat our Swanson's Salisbury steak TV dinners on our little TV trays while watching an episode of *Bonanza*.

Like a lot of Lutheran women, however, Mom could really bake. She made the best apple pie in the history of the world. The key was a lard-based, flaky pie crust. Her apple crisp, coconut "dream" bars, and tart rhubarb pie were, well, incomparable. My favorite cookie was her modified Russian tea cake. For some reason she used a fork to mash the tea cake dough flat before baking. Maybe that converted the Slav Orthodox goodie into something a Lutheran could eat.

Mom didn't like Sundays either, but then she was not happy with a lot of things. She hated her name—Leola Gilma Stime—so she used Lee. Mom complained that at the age of six her teachers had prohibited her from writing with her left hand—what people used to call the "devil's hand." She liked to think that left-handers were especially gifted, like Leonardo da Vinci and Michelangelo, and Presidents Gerald Ford, George H. W. Bush, and Bill Clinton. Although she was

2. My folks, Leola Gilma Stime and Oscar Alfred Anderson, at my wedding to Kristie in 1991, which Dad officiated. Dad was 5'6" and Mom 5'2". Randy and I were inexplicably over 6'2". Courtesy of the author.

not a fan of Ronald Reagan, she knew that he was another left-hander who was forced to write right-handed.

Mom loved to go dancing, but she never got Oscar to go. Music, except for hymns, wasn't in his cold Norwegian soul. Later in life she challenged his Lutheran theology, which did little for the pledge "'til death do us part." Mom rejected biblical teachings about the proper role for women, especially Saint Paul's take: "Women should remain silent in the churches. They are not allowed to speak, but must be in submission, as the law says."

Lee was not going to "be quiet" as Paul enjoined. She was one of the many middle-aged women who fully embraced the women's movement in the 1960s but unfortunately didn't benefit from it. She was a voracious reader who never had the chance to go to college. In twenty-first century America, Mom would not have ended up a church lady.

Mom was a dutiful but begrudging preacher's wife. She followed Dad to the parishes and the college he served, from

Minneapolis to Moorhead in 1954 and back to Minneapolis in 1963. Those were not her roots: she was born in Sinai, South Dakota, and during the Depression her family moved to Chicago, where at an early age she had to go to work to help support the family. Maybe it was because her family had those hard times that Mom had a big heart for the down and out. The bums in Moorhead, as folks used to call them, had marked the fence behind the parsonage as a place to get a handout. Mom always made them sit outside on the picnic table while she fixed them a bologna sandwich.

Mom was four years old when her mother, Emma, died of the Spanish flu, just after she had given birth to her last daughter, named Emma in her honor. Mom never got over the loss. Little Emma was sent off to live with an aunt and uncle. Some fifty million people around the world died of the flu after World War I, the worst epidemic in modern history. A hundred years later the coronavirus hit the world again; although it was devastating, the world health organizations were better able to limit the number of deaths.

Freudians would have had a field day with my mom. Her father, Robert, remarried shortly after Emma's death; many times Mom told us about her stepmother's insistence that Leola call her "Mother." "You're not *my* mother," Mom shot back defiantly.

In 1996, eight years before she died, Mom wrote a letter to her long-dead mother, penned left-handed, not right-handed as she had been taught in school. The letter is a chilling account of her mother's deathbed:

Dear Mother:

It hurt when your voice was stilled. The voices I heard
then were sobbing voices, hysterical sobbing voices of
your husband and my dad. He would not be comforted . . .
could not be because everyone else was sobbing too.
Almost everyone was sick, like you were. Everyone seemed
frightened, I was so scared and no one seemed to notice. I

couldn't find anyone who would hold me—and mother, you were so quiet. They took you away then. What was to become of us? What was to become of me?

And after you rested in your coffin in Grandma's parlor for a few days—and that was scary too for me—they buried you in the ground on a cold, wintry day in the West Church Cemetery of Sinai, South Dakota. Some flowers I still don't like to smell.

Thank you, Mom. I had a good cry and feel better. Talk to you later–

Your eldest daughter,
Lee—love you.

Mom never talked about her father, Robert, which is my middle name. There is some speculation that he had a nervous breakdown after the family left the farm for Chicago. He died when I was very young, but I remember the smell of the flowers at his funeral in Sinai. Mom and I shared the association of roses with death.

Somehow the South Dakota farm stayed in Stime hands. After Robert died, his three girls, Leola, Edith, and Emma, inherited it. Edith and Emma sold their piece, but Mom held on to hers until she died. I always wondered why. After reading the letter to her mother, I understood. South Dakota was in her heart—a cherished link to her mother's memory.

Mom was never comfortable in her role as the minister's wife. Dad maintained a proper Lutheran household, practicing the Babbittry (without the materialism) that Sauk Centre, Minnesota, native Sinclair Lewis satirized in his 1922 novel. On the way to our lake cabin from Minneapolis, you can take I-94 west to Sauk Centre and then north on Highway 71. One time a friend and I stopped at a Sauk Centre convenience store on Main Street, which pays homage to Lewis with huge street signs that read, "The Original Main Street." My friend said to the young clerk, "It must be cool to live in the town where Sinclair Lewis was born, and to work on Main Street."

"What?" she answered.

"You know, Sinclair Lewis, the author who wrote *Main Street* and *Babbitt*?"

"Who?"

During his lifetime Lewis was vilified in Sauk Centre and other small towns in America for his indictment of petit bourgeois hypocrisy, so maybe the young woman's ancestors had never spoken of the turncoat. But you would have thought that one of his books would have been on her high school English reading list.

No swear word was ever heard in the Anderson house, and we did not take the name of the Lord in vain. All the Anderson kids had to take piano lessons from Mrs. Smaby, a doughty old woman who had us play Schubert and Haydn. Boring! But then that was part of a proper bourgeois upbringing. Mom always had the house in perfect order lest some parishioner dropped by. We often heard the old adage, "Cleanliness is next to godliness." We had to make our beds. I think all of my siblings still do, but I'm the black sheep on that count.

We didn't even have traditional playing cards in the house. Those Catholic kings, queens, and jacks were all involved in illicit gambling, another no-no. The only cards we had were from a game called "Rook"; the cards had four suits of various colors and were simply numbered from one to fourteen.

And, of course, there was no alcohol anywhere. As a kid I thought that *beer* was a bad four-letter word, and that people who drank it were sinners. Later on I could never figure out why Protestants pushed Prohibition; didn't Jesus turn water into wine? Mom and Dad entertained a lot, but they served only soft drinks and coffee. In their later years I would bring wine to a family dinner. Dad never had more than a small glass. Mom got tipsy on a couple of small glasses.

The Holy Ghost scared me when I was a kid, but eventually I had trouble believing that Jesus had fed multitudes with a couple of loaves and fishes, and that God, according to the Book of Daniel, had saved Shadrach and friends after they had been shoved into the furnace. It was like what my favorite Uncle Gordon, a droll theology teacher at St. Olaf College, once said, "Wouldn't it be great if it were all true?" To Dad's credit, when we grew up he did not particularly care if his kids were practicing Lutherans. A year before he died he wrote me that "parents cannot always pass on their piety, but they can provide an <u>education</u> and the <u>freedom</u> to pursue it." I guess that is essentially what Lutheranism and its emphasis on the grace of God is all about.

Dad remained true to his faith, but that was the core of his identity. As a kid he would play a minister, just like his dad, making the neighboring kids participate in a wedding or a funeral over which he would preside. I just couldn't believe in the miracles, especially that Mary was a virgin, or that Jesus—a Jewish carpenter—was the Son of God, or that he beat death for my sake. If Jesus were born today, I'm not sure that people would believe the tales that Matthew, Mark, Luke, and John later told. What a huge leap of faith. I think that Jesus had a lot of good messages, but that's about it. Today he would probably be a motivational speaker.

Mom blamed the advent of television for splitting up the family, and she was right. Randy and I were always playing sports or watching some game. Mom tried to convince us that she had been a big Cubs fan because her stepmother used to take her and Edith to Wrigley Field on Ladies Day. We knew better because Mom never sat down to watch a game with us, even when I managed to get sick and stay home from school to watch the afternoon World Series games on TV. Aunt Edith *did* take to the game, watching her beloved Yankees on TV until she died at the age of ninety-two. My older sister, Donna, had little interest in playing or watching games, except to hero-worship the Moorhead High School Spuds' football and basketball stars. Sadly, sports were something girls didn't have the chance to do.

Randy and I wolfed down the Sunday meal Mom had made and ran to watch whatever ball game was on the "boob tube," as she called it. On Sunday we didn't have to suffer through postmeal devotions. In the winter we watched the NBA game of the week, which usually featured the Boston Celtics playing on their peculiar parquet floor. My childhood hero was Bill Russell, the great Celtic center who won more championships than any other player in NBA history. Russell and the Celtics won eight straight championships from 1959 to 1966. I think I cried the night the Philadelphia 76ers ended the streak. I will always remember Russell reminding an admiring reporter, "We are grown men playing a child's game." As an African American child confronting overt racism in Louisiana, and as a player in Boston and on road trips to the Jim Crow South, Russell knew that there were more important challenges in life than a basketball game.

By the time I began to follow sports in the late 1950s, the Lakers had moved to Los Angeles. Randy was four years older, and because he had gone to Laker games at the old Minneapolis Auditorium, he was a big Lakers fan. Randy thought his impish little brother simply rooted for the Celtics because he still liked the Lakers. But, like most kids, I was just rooting for the winner. The Celtics beat the Lakers in seven championship series in the 1960s, and won eleven titles between 1957 and 1969. Randy was a Lakers fan until the Larry Bird era. He lives in Tinseltown now, but hates the transplanted Lakers and the franchise's claim to seventeen championships. Five of those were in Minneapolis, doggone it.

The NBA was struggling in those days. Most of the play-offs were not even telecast. Randy and I strained to listen to NBA play-off games on a faint signal from the St. Louis Hawks' powerful KMOX 1120 AM radio station. I remember the elation I felt one late night in 1962 when the Celtics beat the Lakers in the seventh and deciding game, 110–107 in overtime. The Lakers' sharpshooter Frank Selvy, who once scored one hundred points in a game for Furman College, missed a last-second twelve-foot jumper that would have won the game for the Lakers in regulation. Randy has never gotten over it.

I loved the Celtics, guys named Satch Sanders, Bailey Howell, Clyde Lovellette, K. C. Jones, and "Jungle" Jim Loscutoff. During one televised game the basket support broke, and the Celtics had Loscutoff, a lumbering giant from the University of Oregon, reach up and put it back in place. I was mesmerized by Bob Cousy's passes and dribbling, and I tried to emulate Sam Jones's deadly bank shots.

On autumn Sunday afternoons there was one NFL and one American Football League (AFL) game on TV, starting at noon. Saturday Gopher football games were rarely telecast. If the Sunday games were on at the same time, I sat next to the black-and-white set and flipped the dial on Randy's command, trying not to miss any plays of either game. We broke the plastic channel dial on every TV we owned, so we had to use a pair of needle-nosed pliers to change the channels. The invention of the vise grip was a big tech improvement because we could just clamp it on as the channel changer.

To this day Randy claims that he's the greatest remote controller of all time, and now it's the DVR. He can toggle between numerous DVR'd games without breaking the "cone of silence," as we call the dicey attempt to stay ignorant of the outcome of a game that is already over in real time (the "cone of silence" is a reference to a goofy bit from the 1960s TV show *Get Smart*). The secret is to keep your eyes averted from the crawl at the bottom of the screen that gives the scores and not to take any texts or phone calls during DVR'd games.

My wife, Kristie, is alone among her friends as a Minnesota Wild hockey fan. She doesn't read the sports page, so she can DVR a Wild game and stay in the cone of silence for days. She has learned about not tipping me off to the outcomes of games; once I was videotaping the sixth game of the 1997 NBA championship between the Chicago Bulls and the Utah Jazz. The Bulls were up 3–2 in the series. When I called her to make sure there was enough tape to cover a possible overtime, she said the game was over. "Are you sure?" I asked. "Yes," she replied. "They are showing some guys with hats on in the locker room." Of course I knew that the Bulls were celebrating their win and the championship. It is really tough to stay in the cone of silence these days with everyone getting updates on their apps. I have none of those, but friends who do always spill the beans.

With so few games on during the early days of television, some great moments in sport were indelibly impressed on our young minds, like Baltimore Colt Alan Ameche's short touchdown run to win the NFL championship in overtime against the New York Giants. Or Pittsburgh Pirate Bill Mazeroski's walk-off home run (a term that didn't exist back then) to beat the Yankees in the seventh game of the 1960 World Series. Or Celtic John Havlicek intercepting the Philadelphia 76ers' inbounds pass in the last seconds of the seventh game of the 1965 Eastern Conference Final and Celtics broadcaster Johnny Most croaking over and over, "Havlicek steals the ball! Havlicek steals the ball!"

After we moved back to Minneapolis in 1963, Dad often took us for the Sunday meal at his mother's house on Branston Street in St. Paul, which sat at the top of a huge hill across from Luther Seminary, where her husband, Reverend A. B. Anderson, had taught. When Dad was a kid, if A.B.'s Model T wouldn't start on a cold day, he and his younger brother, Norman, would shove the car down the hill and A.B. would pop the clutch to start it.

Gertrude Anderson was a widower. A.B. had died long before I was born of pernicious anemia, one of those diseases that are no longer fatal today. As the eldest son, Oscar dutifully took care of his wheelchair-bound dad. Shortly before Mom died in 2004, Dad sent me a letter thanking me for "your willing concern for your octogenarian parents. I think I told you what my dad used to say when I tended to him in bed, lifted him into his wheelchair and our car, drove him to his work. . . . 'Remember the promise attached to the 4th Commandment—honor your father and mother and it will be well with you and you will live long on the land.' Maybe that's how come I have lived so long."

We always had the "minister's meal" at Grandma Anderson's, which was usually some mix of grizzled roast beef, spuds, and carrots in a cast-iron pot, put into the oven before church and taken out after. Grandma Anderson also made a weak broth soup with the same ingredients. Occasionally she would treat us with creamed chipped beef on white bread, a Depression-era food affectionately known as "shit on a shingle."

It took the patience of Job to survive Sundays at Grandma Anderson's. In the summer she wanted Randy and me out of the house, commanding us, "Now you boys go play out of doors." All we had was a tiny park across Branston that had an ancient jungle gym. Randy and I were ballplayers, dammit, not gymnasts. We would bring our gloves and baseball, but there wasn't any room on her cramped street to do anything but play a game of catch. Winter afternoons on Branston were interminable. Granny Anderson had no TV and the only game she had was pickup sticks, which kept us quiet and bored for a while, which is probably what she wanted.

My first organized basketball practices were at Sharp Elementary School. The old brown basketballs we used looked like they came from basketball inventor James Naismith himself. When the bell rang at the end of the day we would dash to the gym to get the one or two balls that actually bounced. I was one of the bigger kids, so I tried to emulate a center like Bill Russell. Shooting right and left hook shots in the key was not the best training for my future as a 6'2" shooting guard.

Sharp's fourth-grade teacher was my first coach. He knew nothing about basketball. He liked to watch us shower though, which I thought was kind of weird. Years later he was charged with sexual molestation and ended up in the joint. Sharp's biggest rival was Riverside Elementary, where one of my friends went to school. Years later he was convicted of insurance fraud and he, too, spent time in the slammer. So much for good, clean small-town living.

I was twelve in 1963 when Dad was offered the presidency of Augsburg College, a small Norwegian-Lutheran liberal arts school in south Minneapolis. I didn't know any better at the time, but moving to the big city was like getting a reprieve from Siberia. It was a life-changing move. God slowly left the prodigal son's life, supplanted by a complete devotion to basketball.

2

City Hoops

Within a few weeks of moving to Minneapolis in the fall of 1963, I got hit up for bus fare, had a ball thrown at me while riding my bike, and a classmate told me he was going to punch me out if I didn't stop kicking his books. But my first impressions of the big bad city soon changed. The kid sitting in front of me in Homeroom 111 at Sanford Junior High School, who had threatened me for barely nudging his stuff, eventually became one of my best friends. Lynn Wagner was into ball games more than I was, and Wags was a great little athlete, even though he had a brace on one leg—the result of polio, the dreaded disease of our age that left so many kids disabled.

Sanford Junior High was a culture shock for a timorous little kid from Moorhead. Education experts know that next to the first few years of life, the middle school years are the most important in child development and identity formation. Hormones run wild, bodies change, and kids can be particularly mean and cruel. Sensitivity is not a characteristic of early teens, and rejection can leave deep scars.

Sanford was a scary place. The school was run like a penitentiary, and most of us lived in fear. The school's namesake—Maria Sanford—was one of the first woman professors at the University of Minnesota around the turn of the century. Sanford is one of only a handful of women represented in the hundred statues at National Statuary Hall in the U.S. Capitol. No one told us that, but then the way the Sanford men treated the students didn't honor her pedagogy in any way.

Every hour when the bell rang we had five minutes to go from one classroom (cell) to the next, so a bathroom run had to be carefully calculated. It was possible to get a pink pass for that, but woe to anyone who was caught in the hall without one of those. Recess was like getting a half hour in the prison yard. The lunchroom was strictly guarded. The inmates marched through the cafeteria line for the daily gruel (hamburger pizza day was special, chow mein day the worst), sat in assigned seats, and dutifully rose to be dismissed. Some of us shuffled up to the auditorium, where for a penny you could see about three minutes of some B movie, like Disney's *Moon Pilot*, with Tom Tryon. Not a few of us randy pubescents sat up straight at the sight of his buxom costar Dany Saval.

A misdemeanor of any sort meant a trip to see the vice principal, who had a tough-sounding German name (so did the principal) and a surly demeanor to boot. I never had to go to his office, so I wasn't sure what went on behind those closed doors, but I suspected that it included corporal punishment because beatings went on right out in the open. These guys had not read Dr. Spock. "Spare the rod and spoil the child" was their theory of child-rearing. No one crossed the grouchy metal shop teacher. The drafting teacher liked to put the Vulcan Death Grip on the shoulder of anyone who looked up from his work. One time our portly math teacher took one poor miscreant out into the hall, where we could hear him getting banged up against a locker. Most of us were lily-livered little kids—at least I was—and oblivious to the fact that our educational institution was run like a stalag. It hardened us, however, to take care of ourselves rather than running to our parents, a counselor, or a lawyer.

Mr. Goldstein's graphic arts class, through no fault of his own, was a little behind the times. We worked on presses that Gutenberg might have used, and our lessons were more of a hands-on history lesson than a marketable skill. We tied up our blocks of type together by hand, carved out soft vinyl printing blocks, slapped some ink on the press, and hand-cranked the roller. I have no idea what manuscripts we produced but it was fun, and Goldstein was a good guy. One time he overheard me saying that some kid had "Jew-ed me." I had *no* idea that it was a slur, and he gently admonished me. Somehow *gypped* is still used without censure, symptomatic of that group's continued marginalization.

Even the English teacher at Sanford could send me into a cold sweat. I was not a likely candidate to become a college professor, because I was deathly afraid of public speaking. Miss Downing insisted that we give presentations on a regular basis. It was all I could do not to feign illness on the days I was scheduled to perform. I had all the self-confidence of a pimply, four-eyed geek.

Ball games saved us from our boring, incarcerated junior high regimen. Despite his bum leg, Wags could still compete with us. Homeroom 111 dominated intramural sports. Our homeroom teacher was a big fat guy we called "The Gut." He was a former wrestler at Iowa who taught phys ed, so of course we had to suffer through a unit on wrestling. He liked to get down on the mat and smother us in blubber. Showering after gym class was mandatory. He and the other gym teachers whacked our nude little heinies with a paddle if anyone was goofing around, like snapping wet towels. Both hurt. The Gut, who ran the intramural program, was proud of his boys and their homeroom win record. The other homerooms complained that he gave 111 preferred seedings and biased reffing.

Minneapolis had no inter–junior high school program, so after school Wags and the boys walked over to Brackett Park near my house to play touch football or three-on-three hoops. We had no place to play basketball in the winter, so we played on my makeshift coat-hanger basket in my basement bedroom. We stunk up the place, but Mom never said a word. She liked having the boys over and plied us with cookies and pie.

By the time we got to high school, Wags's handicap was just too great to play varsity sports. He pitched slow-pitch softball well into his fifties, and is the most avid Vikings, Twins, Timberwolves, and Gopher fan I know, flying the various team flags out the window of his car. He has an encyclopedic memory of games and players: "You remember, Shel, right, when Dewey Winston got a first down in the South High JV game against Washburn? You remember, right?" Nope, Wags, sorry I don't. He has a huge collection of sports memorabilia, including a bobblehead doll of the great Green Bay Packer coach Vince Lombardi. The likeness is a spitting image of Warner Oland from the old Charlie Chan movies.

I went to school with the most infamous Sanford Junior High alum, Jim Janos, who after high school went to Vietnam, lifted weights, changed his name to Jesse Ventura, and became a pro wrestler. In the ring Ventura played the supercool beach bum from San Diego. Part of his shtick was to dis anything Minnesota. After giving up his wrestling togs, Ventura threw his hat into the political ring, using the same bodacious no-holds-barred approach. In his own words, he "shocked the world" by winning the 1998 Minnesota governorship. Donald Trump, who often appeared at pro wrestling venues, may have picked up some of his braggadocio from Ventura.

Needless to say, no one would have picked Janos out of our Sanford pack to become governor of Minnesota. Like President Andrew Jackson's rowdies in the White House, Wags and the Southside boys would go over to the governor's mansion on Summit Avenue in St. Paul to watch our beloved Minnesota Vikings get whipped in a play-off game. Beer cans were everywhere; one time I brought over a six-pack of bottles without twist tops, and Ventura had a hard time finding an opener anywhere in the place. Those brews were a little too highbrow.

When Dad moved the family back to Minneapolis in 1963, he enrolled my older siblings, Donna and Randy, at Minnehaha High School, a private Christian school that he had attended in the early 1930s. My younger sister, Gracia, opted to go there, too. Private schools like Minnehaha had their own little state basketball tournament, as did the Catholic schools, but the state public-school tournament was a big deal. It was played at Williams Arena on the University of Minnesota campus. "The Barn" opened in 1928, and is still one of the most famous basketball venues in the country. Over nineteen thousand fans could cram into Williams, the largest seating capacity of any basketball arena in the world at the time.

Until the early 1970s, when the tournament went to two divisions, Minnesota's three-day boys' high school basketball tournament drew more fans than any other tournament in the country. According to *Minneapolis Star Tribune* columnist Patrick Reusse, "The State High School basketball tournament back then had a bigger impact on the state of Minnesota than a [Minneapolis] Lakers' championship." It was the most coveted ticket in Minnesota sports.

I dreamed of playing in that tournament. Wags and most of my buddies were going to South High, so I nixed Minnehaha. I didn't get Latin and other college prep courses at South, which would have been good training for a PhD, but I got an invaluable street education, all too rare among academics.

South High's early claim to fame was an oak table that students built in shop class to be used at the 1892 Republican National Convention at the Industrial Exposition Building in downtown Minneapolis. Delegates stayed at the opulent West Hotel on Hennepin Avenue, where an elderly Mark Twain stayed in 1895 and a young Winston Churchill in 1901. The oak table was used again at the 1896 and 1900 Republican conventions.

Both the Industrial Exposition Building and the West Hotel are long gone, as is my high school. My 1969 class was the last to graduate from the old South High on Cedar Avenue and Twenty-Fourth Street. The "Heart of the Earth," a low-income Native American housing development, sits on that site today. Because kids knew that South was going to be torn down, a lot of the divided windows were pelted with rocks and the panes were replaced by plywood inserts. The architects of the new South, about a mile away, foolishly decided that delinquents would do the same to the new school, so they built a fortress with tiny slits for windows. The interior has virtually no natural light. Nonetheless South High is one of the best schools in the city today, maybe better than it was in the 1960s.

No one used the word *diversity* in those days, but South had a peculiar mix of middle- and working-class whites, Mexican immigrants, African Americans, and Native Americans. Minneapolis has one of the largest urban Native American populations in the country; the American Indian Movement was founded in Minneapolis in 1968. It wasn't a particularly tough inner-city school. To their credit the teachers really cared about their students.

One of my favorites was phys ed teacher Bill McMoore, who had starred on the South High football team in the early 1940s and was a champion Golden Gloves fighter. A guidance counselor told the young Black man to forget about going to college, but Mr. McMoore ignored that suggestion and went to the University of Minnesota, where he walked onto the football team. Mr. McMoore became an assistant principal at Central High and, later, athletic director for Minneapolis Public Schools. The sixties and seventies were not easy times for public schools. "He was just fearless in terms of facing problems," recalled Central principal Marvin Trammel. "People knew they could rely on Bill. He was tough. That was basically what we needed at the time."

Mr. McMoore was one of my football coaches. After a particularly exhausting drill he would say, "Take a blow, boys." I had never heard that phrase before. If any of his students had a dispute, Mr. McMoore would toss them boxing gloves and tell them to duke it out. Now that's old school pedagogy, but we loved Mr. McMoore.

Minneapolis had two predominantly African American communities centered around North and Central High Schools; a lot of folks in those neighborhoods were angry. African Americans were standing up and demanding political and economic equality, and a place in U.S. history books. As the sad story of slavery, Jim Crow, lynching, and constant humiliation and discrimination at the hands of white America was being told and retold, and facing blatant and repeated discrimination, African Americans became increasingly strident in their calls for justice. Riots erupted along Plymouth Avenue in the summer of 1967. Martin Luther King's assassination a year later was for some the last straw.

We had Black guys on our South High teams, so our games with North and Central never had racial overtones. I did not feel any personal animosity from our rivals. Nonetheless, when white and Black people first met in those days there was always a feeling-out period, as if to determine if one of us was a racist and the other was a militant.

There were two brothers on my team, John and Keith Hardeman. Their older brother, Hilary, had played for South as well. The Hardeman family was a bastion of the Southside community. Their father, LeRoy, was the best basketball player at South High in the early forties, playing on coach Lute Mona's first team. Mona was my coach at South a quarter of a century later. LeRoy was only the second African American to be named All-City. After serving in the U.S. Navy in World War II, LeRoy starred on the barnstorming Harlem Roadkings, modeled after the more famous Globetrotters. According to an article in a March 1952 edition of the *Sioux City (IA) Journal*, the Hardeman-led Roadkings beat a team of college all-stars while putting on a "hilarious exhibition" of their "usual crowd pleasing antics."

After the war LeRoy also played with Footy Hughes and Puzzy Wallace on the Negro team in the annual "All-Nations Tournament" that was held at the original Pillsbury House east of downtown Minneapolis. The gym was packed for basketball games between ethnic-based teams such as the Bohemians, Swedes, and Jews, although ringers abounded and players' ethnicities changed remarkably as they switched teams from year to year. At the championship game in March 1947, LeRoy was the high scorer for the Negroes, but they lost to the "Blackey" Arnold-led Germans, 61–41.

LeRoy was also one of the first African Americans to be inducted into the Minnesota Fastpitch Softball Hall of Fame. He refereed park league softball and basketball games well into his sixties. No one messed with LeRoy Hardeman. If you questioned a call, you got an earful in return and a quick technical foul. Park league basketball games can sometimes get out of hand, but never when LeRoy was reffing. Keith, John, and I might have gotten the benefit of a call or two from their father.

Initially I imagined some hostility from the Hardemans. John was the more outspokenly political of the brothers, while Keith maintained a frigid silence. My first impression could not have been more wrong. Basketball brought us together immediately. John was in fact a very smart, funny, good-hearted guy. Keith was merely shy, which at first I mistook as some kind of animosity toward me. He was a good and gentle soul. After he was named All-City in his senior year, Keith gave his award to John.

The Hardemans were not great basketball talents, but tough, hardworking, lunch-pail type guys who, like me, just wanted to win. I used to call Keith "flypaper" because he was so tenacious on defense. He stuck to you relentlessly. When I played against Keith I had to move my jumper farther and farther out just to get a shot off.

After high school Keith went to community college for a short time and then to a trade school to become a sheet metal worker. I went to Augsburg College in Minneapolis. One of the incongruities of American sport is its traditional connection to school teams. Without a college team Keith had nowhere to play except in city recreation leagues, which hardly rose to the competitive or interest level of college sports. Keith might have made the right career choice, but he had to go to college to play organized sports. It is an anachronistic and unjust system. Other countries have competitive clubs and leagues in which anyone can play regardless of profession, and well into their later years.

Keith and I played pickup basketball together for almost thirty years. In the 1980s I formed an AAU team that barnstormed around the region, playing tournaments and small college exhibitions. The guys always wanted Keith to drive his big, comfy black Cadillac to the games. He babied that ride. Lord help us if he had driven one of his beat-up old "work" cars; the chassis on one of his rust-buckets actually broke in half, leaving Keith's derriere a couple of inches off the road.

For several decades after high school, on spring, summer, and fall Sunday mornings the Hardemans (Hilary included) and I played pickup ball at Elliot Park in downtown Minneapolis, near where LeRoy had grown up. We called it "The Church League." The homeless guys liked to sleep off a Saturday-night bender in the park. Sometimes the bums wanted to play, but we gently escorted them off to the grass to watch. A few times there *were* evangelists in the park on Sunday mornings trying to save those poor souls, but the mendicants watched our games more than they listened to the preacher. They hung around for the free meal that came after the sermon.

The Church League is one of my fondest memories of a half-century love affair with basketball. Without the game, Keith and I probably would never have known each other or encountered each other's worlds. He enjoyed coming over to my place to watch college and pro basketball games with the boys, who called him "Mr. Miller" because of his predilection for Miller High Life beer. In a pinch he wouldn't turn down a Grain Belt Premium, but if my college teammate Brad Olson offered him some harder stuff, Keith would shriek in

3. Keith and John Hardeman taking a blow after a "Church League" game at Elliot Park. That's my sweet Bonneville in the background, a virtual rolling living room, like Keith's Caddy. Courtesy of the author.

his high-pitched cackle, "Brad, get those Wild Turkey shots away from me!"

In 2010 Keith Hardeman died suddenly of a massive heart attack. It was one of the saddest days of my life. I wrote a letter to the Hardeman family, who asked me to read it at his funeral. It was hard to get through that eulogy, which I ended this way: "Keith was one of those rare people who come across our lives and leave us better for having known them. He was such a good husband, father, son, brother, and friend. . . . He blessed us with fifty-eight years of a proud life and magnificent love. That memory will not pass but will live on in all of us." It does.

Carl Lumbly also played on my South High team and was a Church League regular. Carl lived just up the street from Elliot Park, but he had little in common with the African American community. Carl's folks were Jamaican. His father was a traditional strict patriarch; studies and other chores came first, sports a distant third. Sometimes I would pick up Carl for our high school games, not knowing if his dad would let him play that night. Carl was liked by all, and was elected student council president.

After high school, Carl got a full ride to go to Macalester College in St. Paul, one of the top liberal arts schools in the Upper Midwest. When he insisted on living on campus, his father threw him out of the house. After the school year Carl had no place to live, so the Andersons took him in for the summer. Carl went on to a long career in theater, film, and TV. His most notable role was as a detective on the long-running series *Cagney and Lacey*.

Along with teammates like Keith and Brad, coaches are the most important influence in a player's life. I was fortunate to have two great ones: South High assistant basketball coach Eric Magdanz and my college coach Butch Raymond. South's head coach, Lute Mona, was an Augsburg grad and a genial guy, but his innovative 2-1-2 zone defense from the early 1940s was a dinosaur in the new age of accurate jump shooters.

One of Mona's drills did serve me well over the years. In half-court scrimmages he would make us play with a deflated ball—kind of like my cold plastic Voit—making it impossible to dribble. The exercise forced us to pass and learn the art of moving without the ball to get open for a shot. Years later when I was doing high school basketball camps with another coach, we would challenge the top two players to a game of two-on-two, promising that we would not dribble. We beat them every time.

Magdanz led South High to the regional final in 1959, then played for Johnny Kundla at the University of Minnesota, where he set several scoring records. He was a great shooter and offensive guru, but he also taught us how to play tough man-to-man defense.

I played football, basketball, and baseball at South, as did most of my buddies. Playing football was a dumb idea for a slow, 6'2", 155-pound string bean. I wound up on both the offensive and defensive line. As a defensive end, I took it to heart when the coach told me to box the corner on an end run, sending the runner inside of me to be tackled by the inside pursuit. That was fine by me because I didn't have to hit anyone. Magdanz was the line coach and neither one of us knew what we were doing. South's football teams were lousy. I don't think we won a game in my three years there.

The best decision I made was to quit football in my senior year so I could shoot hoops. South went to "modular" scheduling that year, meaning that we had a college-like schedule instead of five or six straight hours of class Monday through Friday. I shot basketball before, during, and after school, and took three showers a day. Basketball became my passion; I was a dork with horn-rimmed glasses, so I didn't think girls were interested in me and I wasn't much interested in them.

My dream of making it to the state tournament was a long shot. The Minneapolis City Conference could not compete with the wealthier and better organized suburban sports programs; Edina, the richest of the lot, won three straight state titles from 1966 to 1968. A city team had not made it to the tournament since 1957; South had not been to the tournament in twenty-five years, when LeRoy Hardeman played for the Tigers.

After the urban riots of the "long hot summer" of 1967, as an inner-city school South got some federal money to run summertime activities to keep rowdies off the streets. Magdanz ran it, so our whole basketball team played all summer. State high school rules stipulated that a coach could not be anywhere near off-season pickup games, so Magdanz told us that if anyone with a suit showed up at the gym we should run into the weight room. Magdanz didn't coach us, but we had three months of additional scrimmages, which gave us a chance to compete with the better-financed suburban Lake Conference teams come tournament time.

After we lost our first three games of my senior year, the team told Mona that we wanted to play man-to-man defense instead of his prized 2-1-2 zone. Magdanz approved, although he didn't say anything. Mona was peeved at our insubordination, but to his credit he gave in. We won nine of our next ten games, beating those preppy kids from Minnehaha Academy by thirty-two along the way. Our summer "weight lifting" made us all better players, but no one imagined we were good enough to make the tournament. The superpowers in the Lake Conference blocked our way. We finished third in the Minneapolis Conference, but beat Minneapolis Roosevelt in the district final to send us to the regional semifinal against Bloomington Lincoln, the Lake Conference champion. Lincoln's all-white starting lineup averaged 6'7", with none under 6'3", the height of our tallest player.

During the Christmas break we had scrimmaged two other Lake Conference teams, Hopkins and Robbinsdale. Robbinsdale featured Minnesota Gopher coach Johnny Kundla's son Dave, who was one of the best players in the state. Both teams waxed us, so I had my doubts about our chances against Lincoln. We did have an advantage, however, having played our district tournament at Williams Arena. The baskets in the cavernous old barn hung in the middle of nowhere, giving a shooter little background for depth perception. We got used to it in our three district games.

We trailed Lincoln by ten the whole game, but their sphincters tightened in the fourth quarter and we tied the game, sending it into overtime. I hit an eighteen-footer at the buzzer to win it. At that point in my life I still thought God paid attention to high school hoops, and I told the *Minneapolis Tribune* that "I prayed it would go in when I let it fly." Lute Mona said that he "was so thrilled he shook." The shot brought my cousin Sharon, who was in the Lincoln band, to tears. She didn't hold it against me; she named me one of the baptismal sponsors of her daughter, Laena, who was born a year later.

We beat the small town of Albany in the regional final to make it to the state tournament. My high school baseball teammate Frank "Baker Boy" Duda wrote in the school news-

4. The 1969 Minneapolis South High basketball team, which won the Region 5 championship and made it to the eight-team state basketball tournament, the first Minneapolis team to go to the tournament since 1957. John Hardeman is number 30, Keith number 34, Carl Lumbly number 21, and the author number 11. Coach Magdanz is second from right. Courtesy of the author.

paper, "South is number 1. There's a new confidence, a new pride, a new spirit, and it's evident everywhere you look." Our favorite history teacher, Warren Kaari, observed, "There's been more school spirit here the past week than there's been in the two years I've been here combined." *Tribune* columnist Paul Foss thought that South had a good chance in the tournament, in part because of our smarts: "70% of the 11-man squad is on the honor roll." I'm not sure who told him that.

After leading the whole game, we lost to Crosby-Ironton in the first round of the tournament. I had twenty-five points going into the last few minutes when one of the other guys on our team (the other starting guard) began launching and missing long bombs. My brother, Randy, and others were really pissed off because it was obvious that he was competing more against me than he was against Crosby. He wanted his points. I was completely uninterested in the consolation game against Ramsey the next day, but my teammate shot his way onto the All-Tournament team, which had probably been his objective from the get-go.

I have no idea why he was more competitive with me than with the teams we played. Before the baseball season that spring he told me that he would outhit me by a hundred points. That really wasn't saying much because I was an all-field-no-hit shortstop. I was pretty slick with the glove and made All-City even though I posted a paltry .230 batting average. He had a mediocre senior year at the plate, too; I remember that he did *not* make good on his promise. But he was a good enough hitter and catcher to play for the Minnesota Gophers, then played a couple of years in the Yankees farm system.

Those basketball games played a key role in bridging the gap among the disparate classes and ethnic groups at South High. Much to my surprise, at our twenty-fifth reunion the alums cited our basketball team's run to the state tournament in 1969 as the most memorable event of their senior year. We were all conscious and proud of our underdog, inner-city identity; we bonded because our basketball team represented the heterogeneity and toughness of the city.

No college coach was interested in a slow, vertically challenged 6'2" guard, even if he could shoot a little. I did not get a sniff from anyone. Choosing a school on the basis of sports rather than for a particular major and career path doesn't make sense anyway, but that's the evolution of post-secondary sports in America. Augsburg College's head basketball coach Ernie Anderson (not related) didn't recruit much, but then he came from an era when Minnesota sons and daughters followed their parents to school—in Augsburg's case, area Norwegian Lutherans. One of my favorite English teachers, Dave Wood, recalled the very first class he taught at Augsburg: "The first time I took roll I called Gayla Wadnisczek's name. In a moment of lightheartedness I said, 'How did a nice Polish girl like you end up in a Norwegian place like this?' 'My father married one,' she said glumly."

Augsburg was founded as a seminary in Marshall, Wisconsin, in 1869, a hundred years before I enrolled. In 1872 the school moved to Minneapolis; two years later the first college students began their studies. The seminary eventually merged with Luther Seminary in St. Paul, where my dad had finished his divinity degree. The college is situated along I-94 and I-35; a chronicle of Augsburg's history is quaintly titled *From Fiord to Freeway*.

Augsburg plays in the Minnesota Intercollegiate Athletic Conference (MIAC). Few basketball aficionados would center Minnesota and the MIAC in the history of basketball, but the land of snow, cold, and water has direct connections to basketball's inventor, James Naismith. Minnesota's early love affair with basketball ran from Springfield, Massachusetts, through the MIAC's Hamline University in St. Paul.

The first intercollegiate basketball game in history was played at Hamline in 1895. Athletic director Raymond Kaighn, who had played in Naismith's basketball games in Springfield, organized a game with the Minnesota State School of Agriculture. Each team had nine players on the court, and dribbling was prohibited. Minnesota whipped Hamline, 9–3.

Around the midcentury Minnesota had top-notch college and professional teams, although they never had the popularity of the Minnesota boys' high school basketball tournament. Once again Hamline put its stamp on college basketball history. From 1940 to 1960, coach Joe Hutton Sr. led the Pipers to twelve National Association of Intercollegiate Athletics (NAIA) national tournaments, winning three (1942, 1949, and 1951).

Although the Augsburg student body was overwhelmingly white Protestant, the house I lived in at Augsburg was a model of diversity at a time when no one used that buzzword. My housemates included a Black guy from Cincinnati who became a noted playwright, a Puerto Rican Lutheran from New York City—probably one of a dozen in the country—and an Italian American from Scranton who lived in the closet (literally).

Frank, the cupboard denizen, had taught with my brother in Monticello, New York, and migrated to Minneapolis with

Randy. When he found himself without a job and homeless, we took him in. This was before all of Scorsese's mob films, so we hoity-toity midwesterners had never heard anyone talk like Frank. We called him Filthy Fuckin' Frank (a.k.a. Frank to the Third Power). He didn't go to Augsburg, but he sat in on some classes, went to all of the football and basketball games, and ate with us at the "all-you-can-eat" cafeteria. Frank could always cadge something off our plates.

Frank never played ball games, but years later he became a fanatical long-distance runner. He always ran in the Twin Cities Marathon, and I would look for his name in the newspaper among the finishers in his age category. I told Frank that there should be a category for chain-smokers. He would have trounced that field.

Another guy in the house came from Cannon Falls, which is on the way from Minneapolis to the Mayo Clinic in Rochester, Minnesota. Brad was undoubtedly one of the smartest kids to come out of Cannon Falls, but he loved to tell stories about "Pete the Crow" and other townspeople who reflected the ignorance and gullibility of his small farming community. In 1954 Emperor Haile Selassie of Ethiopia flew into Minneapolis's Wold-Chamberlain Field airport and took a limousine to the Mayo Clinic (for reasons unknown). Cannon Falls got wind that the potentate's motorcade would come down Main Street, and people lined up to get a glimpse of the Rastafarian Messiah. After all, how often does an emperor and savior come to a little midwestern burg?

Before the emperor arrived, Oscar Palrud and Marv Wedin thought it would be funny to have Wedin impersonate Selassie by putting on a Shriner fez and an ornate Indian blanket (as though anyone from anywhere *close* to the Middle East wore a fez and a blanket in the hot desert?), get in a three-car motorcade, and drive through town horn-a-honking and waving to the crowd. The villagers bought the ruse and went home. Twenty minutes later Selassie's entourage sped through an empty Cannon Falls.

Augsburg is just up the street from Cedar Avenue, known at the turn of the twentieth century as Snoose Boulevard, from *snus*—the Swedish word for tobacco. Frank loved to drink coffee, smoke cigarettes, and hang out at Mama Rosa's Restaurant on Riverside Avenue. A century ago Cedar-Riverside and the nearby Seven Corners area on Washington Avenue had a third of the licensed bars in Minneapolis; it was a notoriously seedy and sinful entertainment district. The parents of one of Augsburg's basketball recruits—a suburban kid of Swedish heritage—wouldn't let him go to Augsburg because it was too close to the evils of Seven Corners. By the 1960s, the neighborhood, which had been devastated by Prohibition, was pretty tame. That recruit went to Gustavus Adolphus, a Swedish-Lutheran school in the small town of St. Peter. In games against Gustavus, which was in the MIAC with Augsburg, we chided him with jibes such as "Who's guarding 'Seven Corners'?" After college he became a good friend and we laughed about it.

Maybe Ernie Anderson figured I would go to Augsburg anyway, because the president's son could get free tuition. A lot of my South High buddies, Lynn Wagner included, went to Augsburg, which was about a half mile away. Ten of the thirty South High honors graduates said that they intended to go to Augsburg. Neighborhood connections were pretty strong in those days, even in the big city.

Butch Raymond was my other basketball mentor. Butch's father had gone to Augsburg, and Butch had played for Ernie on some of Augsburg's greatest teams in the early 1960s. The 1963 team made a deep run into the NAIA national tournament, led by 7'0" Dan Anderson, whose dad had also gone to Augsburg. Dan went on to a short career with the New Jersey Nets of the new American Basketball Association (ABA). The only other Auggie to play in the ABA or NBA was Devean George, one of the handful of D-III players ever drafted in the first round, another MIAC distinction. George won three NBA championships with Kobe Bryant and the Los Angeles

Lakers. Hamline's Vern Mikkelsen won four titles with the Minneapolis Lakers.

Ernie and Butch *did* recruit some of the first-year players on the Augsburg team. Early in my first season Ernie moved two other freshmen, Brad Olson and Gary Ellefson, up to the varsity. Although I was on the freshman team that Butch coached, we practiced with the varsity every day. I hounded Ellefson around the court, determined to outplay him in every scrimmage, which I did. Eventually I went to see Butch about why I couldn't get into a varsity game. It was not his call, and Ernie gave me no playing time, but I did get to sit on the varsity bench. On one road trip to St. Mary's College in Winona, some Catholic hecklers who obviously didn't know that every other name at Augsburg was Anderson yelled at Ernie to put his "son" into the game. I doubled over in laughter, probably ensuring that I would ride the pine for the rest of the season. When our star guard Dick Kelley hurt his ankle in the first half of our last game against St. John's, Ernie gave me a shot, almost as if to say, "Okay, kid, show me what you've got."

St. John's always had good teams. It was tough to beat them up in their little bandbox in Collegeville, Minnesota, a tiny town in the middle of nowhere. St. John's was an all-male school. Those Catholic boys were horny and rabid, especially in the dead of the long winter on the central Minnesota prairie. Their games against St. Thomas College, another Catholic school in our conference, were legendary, and not because of some internecine war between Benedictines and Franciscans. Both schools had "rat packs"—the equivalent of English soccer hooligans and their firms. The core drunks were Johnnie and Tommie football players who clashed before, during, and after the basketball games. Eventually the games had to be moved to the afternoon so the rat packs had less time to get hammered.

In 1972 a 6'7", 270-pound St. Thomas defensive end landed in a Stearns County slammer after a melee at a St. John's–St.

Thomas basketball game in Collegeville. The judge ordered him to stay out of Stearns County for a year, except for the one day the next fall when St. Thomas would travel to Collegeville for the big game against St. John's. The judge knew the football schedule, and was either a very fair man or a Tommie partisan.

The Catholics were not the only besotted MIAC fans. Before becoming a state in 1858, the fair-minded Minnesota territory gave the university to Minneapolis, the capital to St. Paul, the prison to Stillwater, and the mental institution to St. Peter (the apostle would not have appreciated that connection). Little did Seven Corners' parents know that Gustavus students drank *a lot more* than we did at Augsburg. What else was there to do in St. Peter? During warm-ups before one game in St. Peter, a potted Gustie partisan unzipped, pulled out his Swedish meatballs and *prinskorv,* and asked the 7'4" St. Thomas center if he would like a bite. Martin Luther hated the Roman Catholic Church, but he never stooped to that level.

Playing with righteous anger in that last game against St. John's, I scored twelve points in the second half and we won the game. We were out of the play-offs anyway, and that was Ernie's last game. I was lucky that he gave Butch the head coaching job the next year. Little did Butch know what he was getting into, not on the court but off it.

In the fall of my sophomore year several of us, Brad included, showed up to the first practice with longish hair. There was nothing really radical about having long hair in those days. Any kid with a little rebellious streak channeled Dylan, Hendrix, or The Dead. Short hair was still the norm in sports, but it was gradually changing. In the early 1970s Cincinnati Reds general manager Bob Howsam mandated that his players have no facial hair. Owner George Steinbrenner did the same with his New York Yankees, but when the wacky owner of the Oakland A's, Charles Finley, allowed big Afros and handlebar moustaches, and the team won three straight World Series championships, barbershops saw a drop in regular customers. The freewheeling ABA, with its red, white, and blue ball and dominant Black players like Dr. J (Julius Erving) sporting huge H-bomb Afros, the small-town, Indiana image of how a basketball player should look changed. Today few coaches deign to enforce a hair code, although in 2018 an Indiana court ruled that it was illegal for a coach to throw a player off the team for having long hair.

Butch didn't care about our hair, but his old mentor, Ernie, who was still the athletic director, refused to issue us equipment. The civil rights movement was all about judging a person—whatever color or gender—on the basis of one's character. We young white guys framed our protest in those terms, although of course we were all advantaged in the long run. We could cut our hair and get right back into the mainstream.

Butch was from Jasper, a small town in southwestern Minnesota, so one might have expected him to side with Ernie. Butch showed great courage in standing up for us against his boss; he had a wife and two young kids, and it could have meant his job. Eventually we agreed to shorten our hair a little, and we stayed on the team. For the next three seasons Butch and I worked through some good and bad times, but I never forgot his loyalty to us. It was a tight bond borne out of that stand we took together. After our senior year he landed a plum coaching job at Mankato (Minnesota) State, and felt indebted to Brad and me; he named his first son Bradley Sheldon Raymond. What an honor.

Butch was a player's coach, too. As my outside shot got better and deeper, he encouraged me to let it fly. We played a fun run-and-gun game, which the Concordia (Moorhead) College coach derided as "YMCA ball." It was especially gratifying to win in my old hometown, and we beat the Cobbers every time. We didn't heed the partisan (corn) Cobbers' chant to "Fear the Ear," but once some Concordia fans greeted me and my longish locks with shouts of, "Faggot. Faggot." Dad even got a letter from an old acquaintance from Moorhead criticizing our motley appearance. Dad responded in his usual diplomatic way: "I think this hair problem has pretty well cooled down. At the Lutheran Brotherhood tournament at Augsburg in December it was evident that most coaches relaxed on this and many of the other teams had much more sloppy looking players than we have. At least none of our players were wearing headbands. Regardless of what you may think of Sheldon's hair, we think he looks even more handsome with his beard." Dad was being nice; it was not a good look for me.

Ernie let it be known that he was still not happy with our unkempt appearance. In my junior year the Augsburg student newspaper wrote, "Shelley Anderson, once a clean-shaving jock, now plays with a beard to the dismay of the Athletic Department, which frowns on such symbols of radicalism. . . . Shelley is just one of a number of jocks who are ignoring the Auggie short-hair tradition." Much to my surprise some St. Thomas players took the shaggy look to another level. Dennis Fitzpatrick (Fitz) grew a huge beard and shoulder-length hair. We dubbed him "The Woodsman." Tommies point guard Paige Piper grew his hair so long that he had to use bobby pins to keep it in place. They are great friends today, but they have never thanked us Auggies for paving the way.

Losing regularly to the Tommies was a conundrum. I grew up in a house in which there was never any alcohol. The Protestant parson, or his wife for that matter, could not be seen going into the liquor store, or have gossip circulating that the minister served alcohol at parties. Coffee only. We knew the Irish Catholics over there in St. Paul were drinkers and carousers, so it didn't seem fair that they always beat us. Was my Protestant God no fun and a loser, too? We also wondered why Tommie head coach, Tom Feely, was always rubbing his crotch during the game. Fitz told me later that the coach was summoning up God's help through his pocket rosary. I guess it worked, although Feely had the refs in his pocket, too.

We lost by three in our last game at St. Thomas in 1973, but it was an inside job. Down two in the last minute of the

5. We lost this game at St. Thomas, but I used this photo to rib Billy McKee that I broke his ankle with a crossover, and to show "Ennis" (there is no D in Dennis) Fitzpatrick playing his usual help defense. The Tommies took our long-haired look to another level. We called Fitz "The Woodsman." Courtesy of the author.

game, the *St. Paul Pioneer Press* reported, "Anderson stole the ball and raced toward the basket on a breakaway with Piper in hot pursuit. As Anderson went up for the layup, he was hit solidly from behind but the referees ruled that [Piper] simply knocked the ball free." Paige admitted later that he had indeed whacked me.

The biggest win of my three years with Butch and Brad came in the play-offs of my sophomore year when we played Moorhead State, the number one–ranked NAIA team in the country. Once again Dick Kelley got hurt, so I was back in the starting lineup after a midseason benching. Gary, Brad, and I each scored over twenty points—most of them from long range—to beat the Dragons by one. It was such a huge upset that years later the Moorhead coach told Butch that he still couldn't get over that loss. The coach thought that it had been Moorhead's year to win the NAIA title, and that some wild-shooting sophomores from Augsburg had stolen it.

I almost blew that game. I had always been a clutch free-throw shooter in high school and college, but earlier in the year we were up by one against St. John's and I got fouled with about ten seconds left. My folks rarely went to my high school games, but as Augsburg president Dad had front-row seats. As I strolled to the free-throw line I winked at Mom, "I've got this." I missed the front end of the one-and-one and St. John's hit a buzzer-beater for the win. I hadn't choked, I had just clanked it.

We were ahead by one with the ball at the end of the Moorhead game when I got fouled. This time there was no way that I was going to make the front end of the one-and-one; as the saying goes, you can't shoot with two hands around your throat. Moorhead missed a contested five-footer at the buzzer. I don't like thinking about it, because a loss that night would have haunted me today as it did the Moorhead coach. They are just ball games, but they are inflection moments that define you. No one wants to be thought of as a choker. Five years later in West Germany, I did win a game on a free throw after time expired, so that monkey was off my back.

There was nothing memorable about my junior year at Augsburg. The seniors were a bunch of lovable flakes who didn't take the game seriously. Gary Severson was a chunky, 6'3", blond Norwegian from Alexandria, Minnesota. When we lined up for wind sprints at the end of practice, "White Owl" would always "let one"—as we in genteel company used to call a fart in those days—scattering the team. Butch

6. The 1970 Augsburg College "long-haired" basketball team. Coach Butch Raymond is kneeling on the right. My best buddy Brad Olson is number 25. Gary "White Owl" Severson is number 55, and Randy Johnson is number 45. Number 13 is the horn-rimmed author. Courtesy of the author.

just laughed. Randy Johnson got wind of us mocking him for squatting like a duck on his jump shot; we didn't think it would completely discombobulate him. On the morning of our last game of the season our two senior centers entered a pancake-eating contest. I was so mad that I went out and shot three for eighteen, the worst game of my career. I didn't hold a grudge though; one of those centers, "Funky" John Ewert, has been my dentist for decades. I'm not sure how he gets his big mitts into my mouth.

In my senior year we finished second again to St. Thomas. I was named conference MVP. Fitz regularly reminds me of his many Tommie championships (we had none), while I tell him, in jest, that all I cared about was individual laurels. In the semifinal play-offs to go to the 1973 NAIA tournament in Kansas City, we lost by one to Winona State University. We had the ball in the backcourt with two seconds left, but the inbounds pass went to a freshman. I wanted that last shot, even if it was a long-distance heave. Winona went on to beat St. Thomas to go to Kansas City.

I cried after the Winona State game, not because we lost but because I thought that was the last important organized basketball game I would ever play. I never imagined that I would play five more seasons in Europe. I wrote a letter to Hershel Lewis, the star of the Winona team, congratulating him on a great game and their trip to Kansas City. Evidently Winona head coach Les Wottke read it to the entire team. One of the assistant coaches, Thomas Voinovich, wrote me back: "I heard about the letter you wrote to Hershel last week. When Coach read it to us I knew it was from you. I really was not only surprised, but it made me feel that life is really a meaning of how a person takes things [sic]."

I received another letter from a Winona lawyer, who complimented me on my sportsmanship on and off the court. The lawyer also sent a copy to my dad, addressed to Augsburg State College. That was ironic because during the game my brother, Randy, told me that he had overheard some Winona fans wondering why Augsburg was so good. One of the Winona fans answered that Augsburg was a private school with a lot of money to buy players. That couldn't have been further from the truth. We had traveled to Winona—as we did in all road games—packed into the coaches' sedans, and ate our pre-game meal at some greasy spoon. Unlike Winona, which had several players on athletic scholarships, we had none.

We never made it to Kansas City, but I was named to the NAIA All-American team anyway. Lewis was the other candidate from our region. He was a better all-around player, but while Winona was playing games in Kansas City, Butch was in the stands pointing out to the other coaches that I had outscored Lewis both times we had played Winona that year, and that I had scored thirty-six in the one-point playoff loss. With Butch's lobbying help, I was selected for the team and Lewis was left off.

There are three teams listed on my 1973 NAIA All-American Award; I am the last name on the third team, so I may have

7. My last college game, which we lost by a point to Winona State. Winona star Hershel Lewis is guarding me. Contrary to my detractors who said that I never shared the ball, I'm about to pass to Brad Olson. Courtesy of the author.

been the last guy voted in. M. L. Carr of Guilford College in North Carolina, and later of Celtic fame, made the first team. The document was signed by NAIA president Eddie Robinson, the famed Grambling University football coach.

By far the greatest accolade I got in college was being named to Lutheran Brotherhood Insurance Company's "All-

Lutheran" first team. It must have been an inside job because the letter announcing my selection was sent to Dr. and Mrs. Oscar A. Anderson, not to me: "Congratulations on your son's selection as a member of the 1972–73 All-Lutheran College Basketball Squad."

At the end of my last season, Gary Olson of the *Pioneer Press* wrote, "It is doubtful that there are many guards in the country that can average 25 points per game, while hitting 57 percent from the field with most shots coming from what would be the ABA's three-point range. And speaking of the ABA, it's rumored Anderson will be drafted by one of their teams. Why not? Critics of Anderson claim he can't jump, isn't fast and doesn't know the meaning of a pass. They're wrong."

Those pundits were not wrong. No one had recruited me to play college ball, and no pro team came calling. But in the summer of 1973 the new Augsburg coach, Erv Inniger, who had a short career in the ABA, lined up a tryout for me with the Carolina Cougars. The flight to Greensboro, North Carolina, was my first plane trip, on now-defunct Eastern Airlines. The Cougars were coached by Larry Brown, who later won an NCAA championship with Kansas and an NBA title with the Detroit Pistons. His assistant, Doug Moe, coached the Denver Nuggets for many years. The Cougars' best player was former Philadelphia 76er Billy Cunningham, one of the marquee NBA players who had jumped to the fledging ABA.

I had no illusions about making the team, but I thought it would be fun to give it a shot. Brown and Moe ran the tryout like a boot camp to weed out the physically weak. I had avoided the military draft during the Vietnam War, so this tryout was as close to a drill sergeant as I ever got. Fifteen of us scrimmaged twice a day for two hours in an un-air-conditioned gym at Elon College. It was ninety degrees in there with humidity to match. Brown made us play full-court pressure defense, and Moe was all over you if you weren't within bad-breath distance of your man. The winning team stayed on the court and the losing team had to run laps, giving us no rest time between games. Vomit buckets stood at both ends of the court. By the end of the first day the heat and humidity had us all limping back and forth from the dorms, where we lay in bunk beds trying to coax our battered bodies back to life.

Five-on-five scrimmages were not the best way to evaluate us because no one was trying to make other guys look good. I was an off-the-ball player who relied on a pick and a pass to get shots, and there wasn't much of either going on. Brown had to institute a four-pass rule before a team could take a shot. He wanted us to "play the right way," as was his mantra, but after that fourth pass the guys immediately chucked up a shot. I didn't have a chance to make it. Players who have ever been dropped from a pro tryout always claim that they were the last guy cut (who's checking?). Even though it isn't true, I have always joked that I was the first guy cut.

At twenty-two I thought that my serious basketball days were over. I landed a job teaching social studies in Hopkins, a Minneapolis suburb. Inniger, a native Hoosier, asked me if I would be interested in an assistant coaching job at Augsburg, but he stipulated that I would have to shave my beard and cut my hair. I was incredulous that the battle we had fought and won years before was coming up again. I stalked out of his office.

Due to declining enrollments at Hopkins, after three years of teaching I was let go. I didn't let on to the school administration that I was happy to leave. I had no definite career plans, but I knew that I did not want to teach ninth-graders for the rest of my life. As much as I enjoyed teaching, pedagogy at that level was mostly packaging the subject matter to entice students to learn; the material itself was not all that intellectually stimulating.

That pink slip was another turning point in my life. Some improbable basketball peregrinations were in the offing.

3

Playing with Germans

One of the first history books I read as a kid was Quentin J. Reynolds's *The Battle of Britain*, a heroic tale of the Royal Air Force's defense of Britain against the Luftwaffe's blitz in World War II. The British fighter plane "Spitfire" could have been named with a ten-year-old reader in mind. I was mesmerized by the dogfights between the little Spitfires and the German Messerschmitts. I could not comprehend the horrific destruction of London, Coventry, and other British cities, but I was hooked on European history and Germany's role in it. I was twenty-six in 1977 when basketball took me to Hannover, one of the German cities that British and American bombers had pummeled.

I had studied German in high school and college, but I didn't take it seriously. Fräulein Borders, fresh out of college, was our German teacher at South High. She gave us German names. Lynn Wagner was Mannfred and I was Robert, which didn't sound very German to me. Mannfred and I used to toss around a few phrases that we memorized, such as "Wie heissen Sie," "Er geht um die Ecke," and "Du bist ein Dummkopf." I learned the basic grammar. At Augsburg College someone told me that Professor Baltina, an elderly Latvian immigrant, gave no one less than a B in her German classes. I guess she didn't get the message, because I got a C.

My connection to West German basketball was pure coincidence. John Caine played for Macalester College, the egghead school in our conference; in 1976 he got a Fulbright scholarship to study in Hannover. He picked up with the local YMCA basketball team, leading them from the third to the second division. In those days European basketball teams were allowed one foreign player, and most of them were Americans. John's Fulbright was over and he was returning to the States. The team needed some help to stay in the second division.

John's mother was a secretary at the school where I was teaching. She connected me with him, and he suggested that I write a letter to the YMCA's coach, John Simons, an Englishman. Simons was enthusiastic about my joining the club, but the YMCA could not afford to pay me. Ekke Albrecht, the head of the club's basketball division, agreed to provide my room and board and help me find jobs tutoring English to high school students.

Ekke had inherited a printing business from his father. The shop was on the first floor of a building on Friedenauerstrasse. Ekke's parents lived on the second floor, and his wife and two kids on the third floor, where I also had a room. Ekke's mother used to feed me lunch on occasion; afterwards she always offered me a shot of Jägermeister. "It's a digestive," she winked.

Although I am 100 percent Norwegian Lutheran (several generations of Andersons and Stimes had met their spouses in the church), Germany and Germans, Martin Luther not the least among them, had figured prominently in the Anderson household. Augsburg College was named for the German city where the Augsburg Confession was signed in 1555, giving local German rulers the right to decide the religion of their realm. It was the culmination of the first round of the wars of the Protestant Reformation. Coincidentally Dad had been in Hannover in 1952 on a trip as head of the Luther League, the youth organization of the American Lutheran Church.

Dad's sizable stamp collection included images of Germany's colonies, the kaiser, and Adolf Hitler; it included a stamp from Germany's Kiautschou concession on Shandong Peninsula in northeastern China. When I did research in 1995 in Berlin for my book on Polish–East German relations, by chance I stayed with a friend on Kiautschoustrasse. Dad also had a beautiful stamp set of native women from French Cameroons, which had been a German colony before World War I. Germany lost all of its overseas possessions in 1919. We lost those stamps, too. A couple of stamp collectors from Dad's congregation duped young Randy into trading them.

The remains of Dad's uncle Eddie Oscar Anderson lie in an American cemetery at Chateau Thierry in France, killed by the Germans in World War I. Dad kept a card memorializing his service, probably sent from the War Department or a private organization dedicated to honoring the war dead. It read, "In loving remembrance of Pvt. Eddie O. Anderson who gave his life gloriously for Liberty and Democracy on the Field of Honor in Beloved France in the year of our Lord 1918." Those are noble reasons for dying, but when soldiers found themselves in the putrid trenches of northern France they soon forgot those glorious, reverential platitudes. War becomes about survival.

As European cities go, Hannover is not very interesting, but it was a good place to learn German. Hannoverians claim that they speak the purest High German. The German I learned in Niedersachsen was understandable to any other German speaker, while the thick Bavarian, Austrian, or Swiss dialects are not. Some of my high school and college German must have stuck in the recesses of my mind, making it easier to pick it up. After a couple of years, Germans occasionally took me for a native speaker. But it was hard to get rid of the hard *r* of American English; one of my German teammates always kidded me if I said something like "Ich fahre nach Trier" (I am driving to Trier). The German *r* is much softer—a sound I struggled to master.

Hannover, like most north German industrial cities such as Hamburg, Frankfurt, and Düsseldorf, was decimated by Allied bombers during World War II. The indiscriminate bombing of civilians was the most controversial Allied military action of the war. Over 400,000 German civilians perished in a campaign that was of marginal importance in meeting the Allies' stated objective of crippling the German economy; 80 percent of Germany's industrial capacity remained intact at the end of the war, while armament production actually increased until the end of 1944.

Over 1,200 Hannoverians were killed and 250,000 lost their apartments in a night raid on October 8–9, 1943. Hannover's old town was completely destroyed and only a small part was reconstructed after the war. Reminders of the war were everywhere in the city. Older buildings were pockmarked from bomb shrapnel; the new buildings had a cold drab, cement-gray Bauhaus feel. As West Germany slowly recovered after World War II, function trumped form.

The Nazi concentration camp of Bergen-Belsen was about thirty-five miles outside of Hannover. As the Germans retreated from the Red Army in Poland in 1945, they tried to cover up the industrial extermination of millions of Jews by blowing up death camps such as Auschwitz-Birkenau and marching the few remaining inmates westward. The films and photos of concentration camps like Bergen-Belsen were even more horrific because the Nazis just let the inmates starve to death. Some of the first evidence Americans saw of the barbarity of the Third Reich came from Bergen-Belsen—emaciated inmates who were nothing but skin and bones. Tens of thousands died *after* the camps were liberated. The Allies filmed bulldozers pushing piles of the dead into mass graves, images that showed the world the utter depravity of the Nazi regime. Alfred Hitchcock advised on one British documentary; famous Hollywood director George Stevens, working for the U.S. Army, also filmed the horrors of Belsen and other Nazi concentration camps.

I visited two former concentration camps in Germany in the late 1970s, and two Nazi death camps in Poland a decade later. The contrast between the camps in the two countries could not have been starker. The West Germans had sanitized the museums at Bergen-Belsen and Dachau (near Munich); they were freshly painted and tidied up. The Polish death camps at Auschwitz-Birkenau and Majdanek (near Lublin) smelled of rot and death. Sheds at Majdanek were piled up with shoes, eyeglasses, and suitcases just as the Nazis had left them in 1945. The Polish communists struggled to build Poland's economy after the war and did not have the resources or the inclination to whitewash the crimes of the fascist Nazi regime. The West Germans had both. After all, the Germans had started the war that caused tens of millions of civilian and military deaths, and they conducted the largest ethnic-cleansing and genocide operation in history.

The U.S. military and the American public were horrified by the atrocities, and wanted collective punishment of the Germans. The Allies made ordinary Germans walk through the concentration camps to see the piles of emaciated bodies. Shortly after the war, the U.S. occupation authorities began a thorough denazification process in the American zone, targeting ordinary Nazi party members as well as higher-ups. At the end of 1946 the Americans stopped denazifying the general population because West Germans were now needed to build a democratic, capitalist state as a bulwark against communism.

Celebrities who had cozied up to the Nazis and Hitler personally, such as filmmaker Leni Riefenstahl and heavy-weight boxer Max Schmeling, were given a pass. The United States even put scientists such as Nazi rocketeer Wernher von Braun to work on U.S. military and space projects; von Braun developed the Apollo rockets that took American astronauts to the moon. The famous German actress Marlene Dietrich took a different path. She refused to work for the Nazi film industry, defected to the United States, and gave shows for American troops during World War II. When she visited West Germany after the war, she was greeted with boos and catcalls, and was even spat upon during one appearance in Düsseldorf.

West German business leaders who might have been implicated in the atrocities committed by the Third Reich could bury their past. The Soviets harped on the fact that companies such as Siemens, Mercedes-Benz, Bayer, and Krupp continued to operate with some of the same bosses who had profited from the war. In my second year in Germany, I did some research in an Osnabrück archive on local Nazi Party members. Several businesses in the town bore surnames that showed up on Nazi Party lists. When I met older Germans, I could not help but wonder if they had been in the Hitler Youth, the Nazi Party, the Wehrmacht, or the ss. I rarely asked. Obviously, Germans wanted to move on.

In the fall of 1977 I flew from Minneapolis to Luxembourg on Icelandic Airlines to begin my semi-professional basketball career. Icelandic was a thrifty way to get onto the continent. The flights always stopped in Iceland late at night, which was a nice break in the long flight. I have heard that Iceland is a beautiful country, but I never saw anything but the inside of Keflavík Airport.

John Simons picked me up in his beat-up old Volkswagen. I immediately bonded with the droll, hard-drinking Englishman from Doncaster. John's German was impeccable, but we spoke English. That was the only exception to my resolution to speak German exclusively, even if it was painstakingly rudimentary at first. We had a mutual passion for basketball and music, although I knew a lot more about the former and John more about the latter. He was a huge Boston Celtic fan, like me. His favorite player was John Havlicek, the Celtics' prolific scorer and tenacious defender in the sixties and seventies. We both liked the quirky band Talking Heads and the new group Dire Straits, whose hit "Sultans of Swing" showcased the brilliance of guitarist Mark Knopfler. John and I saw Dire Straits in Hannover for one of their first concerts. They played about ten songs and left the stage. The crowd was going wild for an encore, but the band didn't have any more songs, so they played "Sultans" again. The crowd loved it anyway.

John was at home in Hannover, where he could have a pint or two with British soldiers stationed there. Hannover was in the British zone of occupation after the war. We could pick up British armed forces radio and nighttime disc jockey Alan Bangs, whose "Night Flight" program turned us on to latest in rock 'n' roll. Those were the days of the DJ who played his favorites instead of a mandatory computerized playlist. If you liked the DJ, he was your personal tastemaker. Now playlists come from a faceless algorithm.

John was a travel agent by day, coach at night, and on weekends the lead singer in a rock 'n' roll band called The Boobs, a reference to their collective musical talents rather than to a woman's anatomy. John was a Jagger wannabee without the voice, the energy, the libido, the happy feet, or the backup band. That didn't matter to the clientele at the small German bistros, who accepted bad rock 'n' roll as long as it *was* rock 'n' roll. If The Boobs played a scruffy facsimile of "I Can't Get No Satisfaction," that was enough. John used to tell me that Marlene Dietrich couldn't sing either. But she was über cool. John's band? Not so much.

Simons's basketball acumen was limited to what he had learned from a public school teacher who had probably read a book about the game. Any Englishman who played basketball rather than soccer or cricket was rather daft anyway. To his credit John let me map out our plays and help run the practices. During games John would make an observation here and there and yell an occasional "Oh, come on" at the refs. If I played well he might mumble, "That was pretty good," but most of the time he offered snide critiques of my play, all with an impish smile. I loved playing for him.

John was my introduction to the English attitude toward sport. In the mid-nineteenth century England refined the rules of soccer—the most popular game in the world—and cricket and rugby, which the Americans revised into baseball and American football. The middle and upper classes played these sports as a way to inculcate Victorian values in their young men. Sports were not to be played for money, but as a leisure-time activity. Teamwork and good sportsmanship were supposed to be as important as winning. A pint, a port, or a nice scotch after the game didn't hurt either.

At the end of the century the amateur tradition in British sports was challenged by working-class soccer clubs. Workers did not have the leisure time to play on club teams on a regular basis, and could ill afford to take off work, so clubs began to pay players. Nonetheless the amateur was the ideal British sportsman. John took sport for a jolly good time, so we didn't practice very hard. As Godfrey Rampling, a British relay runner at the 1936 Berlin Olympics said to his teammates about practicing for the big race, "'Look here, chaps, we really ought to practice some baton changing.' But we soon got bored and packed it in." I was the American pit bull wanting to win at all costs, while John looked forward to the postgame libation. The Germans on our team followed orders and could go either way.

On the drive from Luxembourg to Hannover on my first day in Europe, John and I toured wineries along Germany's picturesque Mosel Valley, where I got a quick lesson in Kabinetts, Spätleses, Ausleses, and other German Rieslings. I never drank much beer or wine in college, but the German versions were so much better. A lot of German immigrants started breweries in America, and one wonders what happened to their watered-down suds. And until the late twentieth century, few Americans knew good from bad coffee or wine either. My folks and their friends drank their Folgers or Maxwell House black—a tasteless, bitter brew.

Jet-lagged and a little hungover, I had my first practice with the team the day after I arrived. John's drinking ritual became a pattern throughout the season. He often took me out the night before a game to get me stewed, and when I begged him not to buy me yet another pint his reply was always the same: "Anyone who can't play hungover is not worth his salt."

8. My Hannover coach John Simons and his bandmate Walter Peters at the Deutsches Eck in Koblenz during our March 2018 reunion wine tour. That's Kaiser Wilhelm I on the horse. Simons, a former travel agent, mistakenly booked our hotel for April. Courtesy of the author.

During one break in the basketball schedule, John, his roommate and fellow Boob Walter Peters, and I drove to Rhine wine country. Walter was a jovial, portly high school music teacher whose passions were wine, women, and workers of the world. He was a walking Hegelian dialectic—a committed Marxist on the one hand, and an opulent, decadent bourgeois materialist on the other.

Comrade Walter spoke with great enthusiasm about his many trips to Havana and the virtues of Castro's socialist state, without acknowledging that Cuba received billions of dollars in subsidies from the Soviet Union or that it was a dictatorship. He had more trouble defending the East German socialist state, which he visited only a few times, mostly on day trips to East Berlin, where he could buy some cheap music scores, courtesy of the command-economy discount. The drab Marxist capital should have changed his thinking, but what soured him on Soviet politics in the long run was Moscow's suppression of the Czechoslovak communist party reform movement in 1968. Coincidentally, Walter was in Prague when the Warsaw Pact troops marched in.

Walter's family history, and his cognizance of the horrors that imperial and then Nazi Germany had inflicted on the world, explain his leftist weltanschauung. Like many Germans who lived through the volatile twentieth century, Walter's parents, Walther and Margarete, and grandparents survived a series of extraordinary events. In August 1914 Walter's grandfather Heinrich Ahlvers was on the ocean liner *Kronprinzessin Cecilie,* sailing from the United States to Germany. Heinrich's wife was pregnant with Margarete and had stayed behind in Bremen. World War I had started by the time the ship—laden with gold bullion—reached the English Channel, and it turned around back to the United States. Heinrich and the rest of the German crew were free to move about in neutral America, but they were eventually interned after the United States entered the war in April 1917. The United States commandeered the ship and turned it into a troop transport, the USS *Mount Vernon.* At the end of the war, in 1918, Heinrich was finally reunited with his wife and child.

In 1937 twenty-three year old Margarete took a trip to Madeira on the *Wilhelm Gustloff,* a cruise financed by the

Nazis' highly popular Kraft durch Freude (Strength through Joy) vacation program for average Germans. As the Red Army was entering East Prussia in early 1945, Walter's mother, along with millions of other Germans, wanted to escape to the West. Margarete tried to get on the same *Wilhelm Gustloff*, but the ship was full and she never made it on board. A Soviet submarine sank it on January 30, killing over 9,300 people, the worst disaster in maritime history.

Walter's father, Walther, was born in Westphalia in 1914 and received his Abitur (high school graduate degree) on January 31, 1933, the day after Hitler came to power. Walther studied law under the infamous jurist Carl Schmitt, who became a prominent member of the Nazi Party. Schmitt justified Hitler's murder of opposition figures during the so-called Röhm-Putsch (Night of the Long Knives) in 1934 under the principle of *Führer-Ordnung*; he called the notorious Nuremberg Laws of 1935, which restricted Jewish rights, a "Constitution of Freedom" (*Verfassung der Freiheit*). Walther did his army training with Karl Carstens, the future president of West Germany.

Walther left Nazi Germany in 1937 and moved to Danzig (Gdańsk), where he was a radio newscaster. He witnessed the German bombardment of Polish installations at Westerplatte on September 1, 1939, and was one of the first to broadcast the outbreak of World War II. He was then forced to serve in Josef Goebbels's propaganda ministry as a war correspondent in France, in North Africa (with Rommel's troops), and on the Wehrmacht's march to Baku in the Soviet Union. Toward the end of the war he barely escaped getting trapped in Crimea with the retreating German troops. He was ordered to Berlin in January 1945, but defied the orders. With a Kalashnikov in hand in case he ran into the ss, Walther headed to the Harz Mountains to see his newborn son Wilfried (meaning "desire for peace"), but was captured by the U.S Army and sent to a POW camp in northern France. After the war he became a journalist in Lüneburg, near Bergen-

Belsen, where he covered the trials of the camp's war criminals. What a life, only three decades into it.

On the trip to the Rhine in 1978, John, Walter, and I—the Tommy, Jerry, and Ami—stopped at winery after winery, sampling vintages along the way. During one dinner we took the sommelier's blind wine tasting test. Walter, who fancied himself a connoisseur of German white wines, misidentified every one. He bought so many cases of wine that I thought the rear shocks on the car were going to collapse. John and I made fun of Comrade Walter driving his Mercedes home nose up—overloaded with expensive wine. Some socialist.

Part of John's job as a travel agent was to scout British bed-and-breakfasts for his German clients, so the three of us took another trip to England and Wales. John knew some of the most famous pubs on the British Isles; our tour consisted of driving from one to the next, all calculated so as not to miss, as John put it, "valuable drinking time." In those days British pubs were open for only a few hours in the afternoon and evening; John had our bar-hopping perfectly timed. The weather was just right for John's pub crawl—cold, gray, and rainy. A warm fire, a friendly proprietor, a pot pie, and a couple of pints and ports put us in a merry mood. I even brought along a couple of Agatha Christie novels. On occasion we "chatted up a few birds."

These trips seemed to be John's tests to see if I could play basketball without practicing. One time his travel agency gave him two round-trip flights to Mexico City for about fifteen bucks each. My American girlfriend happened to be vacationing in the west coast city of Manzanillo, which as the crow flies looked to be about three hundred miles from Mexico City, so I went along. My girlfriend did not know we were coming, I had no clue where she was staying, and John and I had no idea what we were doing.

The drive from Mexico City to the west coast turned out to be a grueling sixteen-hour, serpentine marathon through the mountains. Our rental car had no air-conditioning, so

John, a pale, fair-headed Englishman, burned his left arm to a crisp on the way. We also didn't know that Manzanillo was a big city and that it was the Easter holiday. All of the hotels in downtown were full, but we finally found a place along the beach that catered to Americans. John went to sleep while I scouted out a couple of nightclubs in the area. As I walked into the first one, I heard a shriek, "Shel!" Improbably, I had found her.

After a week in the blistering Mexican sun, which John tried to avoid like Dracula, we drove the sixteen hours back to Mexico City and got on the ten-hour return flight to Frankfurt. I had to play a road game in Dortmund the next day. John sat on the bench laughing as I played through Montezuma's revenge. I had twenty-five and we won that game, so I guess I was worth my salt.

One of the teams in our league was Charlottenburg in West Berlin. Traveling through East Germany to play them was my first foray behind the Iron Curtain. Growing up under the cloud of atomic Armageddon, I had always been intrigued with this alien world. Why were we so afraid of the Reds? The editors of my high school yearbook asked all the seniors, "What you will do in ten years?" I wrote, "Visit Moscow."

I was enthralled with the Olympics and the epic battles between Soviet and American athletes, between good and evil, freedom and dictatorship. The 1960 Rome Olympics were the first games televised in the United States. The drama of American high jumper John Thomas (the favorite) losing to Soviet Robert Shavlakadze, long jumper Ralph Boston beating Igor Ter-Ovanesyan, and decathlete Rafer Johnson besting Vasili Kuznetsov was compelling, as was the speculation (unfounded) about the true gender of Soviet track-and-field gold-medal winners, sisters Tamara and Irina Press. The Olympics were really fun to watch in those days because more gold medals ostensibly proved the superiority of one political system over the other. Plus, the Soviets were (unfairly) portrayed as cold, robot-like products of a professional sports machine, while American amateur athletes represented individual pluck and perseverance.

I never made it to Moscow, but I was a frequent visitor to Soviet Russia's ugly socialist offspring, the German Democratic Republic (GDR). The border dividing West and East Germany was a kilometer-wide no-man's-land with barbwire fences and concrete barriers. The Iron Curtain was intimidating. Our bus had a long wait on the West German–East German border, and another lengthy delay on the East German border with West Berlin. As the capital of Nazi Germany, Berlin had been divided into four occupation zones after World War II. Until the East Germans walled off East Berlin in August 1961, Berlin was an open city. Thousands of East Germans a month (three million total in 1961) were leaving the GDR through Berlin; as an island of democracy and capitalist prosperity in the middle of the GDR, West Berlin was an obvious contradiction to propaganda proclaiming the superiority of the communist way of life. The GDR leaders finally convinced the Soviets to allow them to build a wall to keep East Germans in. The East German government called it the Antifaschistischer Schutzwall (Anti-fascist Protection Wall) to keep westerners and their fascist influences out. Except for die-hard communists, East Germans knew better; hundreds were shot trying to get over the prison wall to freedom in West Berlin.

West Berlin was the Achilles heel of NATO. Surrounded by Warsaw Pact forces, there was no way to defend it. Nikita Khrushchev, who was Soviet premier when the Berlin Wall went up, used to say that if he wanted to make the West squirm all he had to do was squeeze the balls of West Berlin. President John F. Kennedy did not challenge the Wall as long as the Soviets did not infringe on the rights of the western Allies in West Berlin. For Kennedy the Berlin Wall lessened tensions over the status of the former German capital.

The Berlin Wall and the East Germans' fortified border separating West Berlin from the GDR were constant reminders to West Berliners that they were in a no-man's-land, and that the GDR controlled access to the city. Most native West Berliners stayed put, but the city had trouble keeping young people or attracting West Germans to move there. One of the guys on our team claimed residency in West Berlin because West Berliners were not obligated to serve in the West German armed forces.

On the way to play Charlottenburg, I was taken off the bus by the no-nonsense East German border guards and told that, as an American, I would have to pay an extra fee for transit through the GDR to West Berlin. Those border guards must have been trained in a school for the surly; their sour demeanor only added to the portent of entering the socialist camp. For the first time in my life, I felt the power of a police state. Whatever problems western countries had, at least most of their citizens were free. As my dad used to say, count your blessings.

The day after the Charlottenburg game some teammates and I got one-day visas to get into East Berlin. That part of the city was actually more interesting than the modern architecture of West Berlin. Much of Berlin's beautiful old center ended up in the Soviet zone. The broad boulevard Unter den Linden started at the Brandenburg Gate, which was the most prominent landmark along the Berlin Wall. The Reichstag—still crater-faced from wartime bombardment—stood a few hundred meters inside the wall on the western side.

On Unter den Linden to the east stood the Berlin State Opera, the Berliner Dom, Humboldt University, and other neoclassical buildings built by the Prussians in the eighteenth and nineteenth centuries. The facades were still damaged from the Soviet assault on the city in 1945. The Reich Chancellery and Hitler's bunker were long gone. After blowing up the remains of the old Prussian Stadtsschloss (City Palace), the East German government built a new Palast der Republik on the spot in the hideous, socialist-functionalist style of steel and glass. Its drab, boxy modernism, along with the renaming of the Schlossplatz to Marx-Engels Platz, mocked the Prussians' ostentatious Machtarchitektur.

The one-day visa to East Berlin came with a mandatory currency exchange of twenty West German marks (about $10). The GDR hungered for hard currency, and the one-to-one exchange rate they commanded from visitors to the GDR was a scam. The exchange rate on the street was about one West German mark to six East German marks. The currency black market was ubiquitous in the Soviet bloc, but changing money on the street in East Germany was risky. The East Germans, true to the Prussian stereotype, took the socialist order more seriously than any of the other Soviet satellites. One had to worry that changing money on the street in East Berlin would be reported to the authorities. After the demise of the GDR in 1990, it was revealed that every fifth East German was cooperating in some way with the Stasi—the East German secret police. One theory about why Germans love nudist camps so much is because historically they have lived under authoritarian regimes and strict societal norms. Nudists can let it all hang out.

A decade later when I was playing ball in communist Poland, I was frequently asked to exchange hard currency for zlotys. No one paid any attention to these transactions. Even government officials asked to buy my dollars or marks. I once met a South African student who told me that upon arriving in Poland he had immediately taken his university stipend to a Polish bank, where he had changed Krugerrands into zlotys at the official exchange rate. I calculated that he had lost about $6,000 by changing his money at the state bank instead of on the black market. I didn't tell him.

A few of my Hannover teammates exchanged money on the street and we went to eat at an East Berlin restaurant. Food was heavily subsidized in the socialist states, so with our East German marks we ate and drank at a fraction of the cost of a comparable meal in West Berlin. The food was adequate, but it would have been a luxury meal for the average East Berliner. When we paid the bill, the flinty waitress demanded to know where we had gotten so much East German currency. "On the street?" she asked, and berated us as corrupt western capitalists. She threatened to turn us over to the authorities.

There was no incentive for her or anyone working in a socialist enterprise to provide good service, work hard, or innovate to make the business more efficient and profitable. The cranky waitress would keep her job regardless, and the state restaurant did not have to turn a profit. Socialism doesn't work because it is contrary to human nature. People work for themselves first, their family second, and their community third. Sacrifice for some distant, abstract political entity—in this case the East German state—energized only a very few zealous Marxists. East German workers got a salary set by the state, no matter how hard they worked. No one likes to pay taxes; in the communist system nearly all of a worker's productivity went to the state. Work and goods were shoddy.

Although both states were communist dictatorships, whenever I crossed from East Germany to Poland it was as if I had left a police state for a free country. Most Poles were indifferent to socialism, but the East Germans were determined to create the perfect socialist dictatorship, an even stricter and better version than that of their Soviet mentors. They didn't say it out loud, but the arrogant East German regime was proud that they had constructed the most developed socialist state in the communist world. The East German communists believed that the backward Slavs to the east, especially the Poles, were not up to the task.

Soviet-style communism was the height of social engineering, which rarely if ever works. It was the height of hubris for the communists to think that they could force a new way of thinking down people's throats, at the end of a gun if need be. The extraordinary success of the East German Olympic team epitomized this grandiose Marxist experiment; we know that East German athletes were heavily doped with performance-enhancing drugs. It was a criminal operation, often unbeknownst to the athletes themselves.

I had a nice season in Hannover, and we finished in the middle of the second division. I even got an interview and photo in the *Hannoversche Allgemeine*, the biggest newspaper in town. One of my challenges on the court that year was trying to get the team to think basketball, not soccer. They rarely saw the American game on television, and all of my teammates had played soccer as kids, so their instincts came from that game. They liked to get the ball to the flank on a fast break, like finding space in soccer. After watching them jump out of bounds under our own basket in the hope that one of our guys would catch the centering pass, I finally figured out that they were just crossing the ball into the middle as you would in soccer. I had to inform them that ball possession in basketball is much more important.

The international rules at the time also mirrored soccer. For example there was no inbounds pass allowed under your own basket; if the ball went out of bounds in the backcourt, the referee did not need to touch the ball. You could just grab the ball and inbound it immediately. That really cut down on arguing with the refs.

At the end of the season a player from another Hannover team told me about a new club that had formed a year earlier in the small town of Bissendorf near Osnabrück, a midsize city in northeastern Germany about an hour from the Dutch border. Osnabrück and nearby Münster are famous as the sites of the signing of the Peace of Westphalia in 1648, which ended the devastating Thirty Years' War. Some historians credit Westphalia for ushering in the age of the modern European state system. Osnabrück was the birthplace of the famous writer Erich Maria Remarque, who had studied at the University of Münster. Osnabrück also had a basketball tradition; VfL Osnabrück won the West German championship in 1969, but fell apart in 1972.

9. Scoring a dipsy doodle layup for the Bissendorf Giants over Bayer Leverkusen's center Norbert Thimm, who was a stalwart on the West German national team. On the right is my teammate Tom Norwood (#10) and Leverkusen's John Ecker (#8), who won three NCAA championships with coach John Wooden at UCLA. Courtesy of the author.

After I outscored another American in a tryout scrimmage in Bissendorf, the club offered me the use of a BMW, a nice apartment, and a decent salary. It was not life-changing money, but it gave me the means to travel around Europe in my spare time and to pursue postgraduate studies in history.

Peter, the head of the club, was the son of parents who had fled East Prussia at the end of the war. Like millions of Germans from the East, the family feared retribution from the invading Red Army and resettled in a western zone. Peter was fortunate to grow up in a capitalist, democratic Germany where he was able to make a fortune in insurance. Rumors floated around that he also owned brothels in Düsseldorf.

If there was a poster child for East German propaganda caricaturing the decadent West German bourgeoisie, it was Peter. He was a true glutton; one of the guys on the team called him "Der Dicke" (the Fat Guy) for his ample appetite and beer belly. The nickname stuck. Peter lived in a hillside villa, had several big BMWs, stayed in five-star hotels, ate at fine restaurants, and wore expensive clothing and jewelry. He drove 120 mph on the German autobahns (which was legal), racing up the left lane to tailgate cars ahead of him and flashing his lights for them to move over. He was guilty of road rage before that term existed.

Typical of the West German nouveau riche, Peter sought any ostentatious display of wealth. The Bissendorf club gave him the publicity he craved. I suggested that we call the team the "Giants," and he loved the idea. I ordered Chicago Bulls model uniforms for the team, and he loved that, too. Peter was a big fish in a small pond. The Bissendorf Giants were not the Los Angeles Lakers, but we were the talk of Osnabrück and West German basketball circles. One year Peter rented snow-white Volkswagens for every player.

Peter lavished parties and holiday trips on "his boys." After games he treated the team to a massive buffet and all the alcohol we could drink. After one big win, the local newspaper wrote, "As usual the Fürst [Prince] came into the locker room," referring not to Peter but to bottles of Fürst von Metternich sparkling wine. The opposing team was often invited to the bacchanalia. The Finnish national team took more advantage of the free booze than any other team we played. Evidently alcohol was very expensive in Helsinki. Sometimes when Peter was leaving one of these fests, he would stuff a couple of hundred marks in my pocket and tell me to make sure the boys had a good time. The other American players in West Germany thought that I had one of the best basketball jobs in the country.

Every winter Peter and a couple of his buddies went to Lech, Austria, for a two-week ski vacation. During a break in my first season with the Giants, he took me along. I know I was the only American player to receive an all-expenses-paid ski vacation to the Alps. No other team would have risked injury to its best player.

Peter always stayed in a five-star hotel that was perched on the side of the mountain next to one of the ski runs. We had to park the car in Lech and take a cable car up to the hotel. The view, the air, the skiing, the cuisine, and the wine were all top-shelf. I had never skied, so Peter hired an Austrian ski instructor, who worked me over for six hours every day for a week.

Peter didn't ski much. He had more fun watching the Austrian break me down. Every day Peter would sun himself at the outside hotel bar, buy everyone champagne, and watch the skiers schuss by. When he paid the hotel bill at the end of our stay, he plunked down a huge wad of marks. He was proud of the fact that the stack to cover the bar tab was bigger than the one to pay the bill for the hotel, food, and skiing.

The West German basketball association allowed only one foreigner in the lineup for league games, but for European Cup games teams could play with two. Before my second year in Osnabrück, Peter hired Tom Norwood, a 6'7" power forward from Alabama Baptist who had been playing in West Germany for several years. Tom was the first Black guy from the Deep South I had ever known. He was a soft-spoken, polite, deferential southerner. I always got a chuckle at the stereotypes he had about Black people, such as "Black folks don't like heights," or "Black folks don't like to fly," or "Black folks can't swim." I told him that he was full of shit. On the court Tom reminded me of the guys I had played against at my ABA tryout; he had superior speed, quickness, and spring. When Tom and I played one-on-one I had to move out to twenty-two feet just to get a shot off. He never left Germany; today he is a *Hausmeister* (custodian) at a high school in Ulm.

The next winter Peter took Tom along to Lech. Like me, Tom had never skied, so he got his ski instructor, a petite Austrian fräulein. I can safely say that Lech had never seen a 4'7" ski instructor chasing a 6'7" Black guy careening down the slopes. Peter called Tom "Der Schwarze Lavine" (The Black Avalanche). Tom made us the talk of the town, which is exactly what Peter wanted. One night we were sitting at a bar in Lech when two British jet-setters invited Tom to join them for a drink. He was gone for three days before we saw him again, sitting in a horse-drawn sleigh, grinning ear to ear as he rode by with his arms around the two women. They had helicoptered Tom to Switzerland for a few days of partying.

The Giants held one preseason training camp at an Austrian resort on the Wörthersee. From there we took a day trip to play a team in a small town near Ljubljana, the capital of Slovenia, which at that time was still part of Yugoslavia. Much to our surprise the game was played on an outdoor court. The guys on our team were not happy about this. I thought it was cool to be playing in Tito's communist Yugoslavia. When some Slovenian kids came up to Tom and began rubbing his hand and arm, he asked me, "What the hell are they doing, Shel?" "They've never seen one of you," I chuckled.

In 1979 Peter flew three Giants to Washington DC for the NBA finals between the Seattle Supersonics and the Washington Bullets. We stayed at a suite at the Watergate hotel, which had gained notoriety a few years earlier for President

Richard Nixon's "plumbers" raid on Democratic Party head-quarters. We rented a car and on the way to the game Peter was driving like he did on the autobahn, speeding and tail-gating in the left lane. We got pulled over by an irate cop. As he began to lay into Peter, Peter interrupted, feigning igno-rance of any English: "No understand. To Bullets basketball. Dribble dribble." The cop was so flustered that he let Peter go with a warning. I could barely keep from laughing and blowing my cover. The cop thought that none of us in the car spoke English.

The next year Peter flew the entire team to New York City. He got tickets for a couple of us to drive to Philadelphia for the sixth play-off game between the Los Angeles Lakers and the 76ers. Kareem Abdul-Jabbar was hurt and did not play, but rookie Magic Johnson doubled as point guard and cen-ter and led the Lakers to the title.

Some of Germans on the team were a little nervous about walking around New York City, which in the seventies had a reputation for high crime and urban blight. They asked Tom to show them around, probably because they figured that a Black guy would be streetwise. But the Alabaman was just as awed by the Big Apple as they were. It fell to me to play tour guide. I even took a few of them to play outdoor hoops with the locals, who got a kick of these strange foreigners play-ing an away game on their Harlem home court.

I knew New York City because of a summer job I had in upstate New York in 1972. Between my junior and senior years in college my brother, Randy, brokered a job for me as a cabana boy at the Concord Hotel near Monticello, New York, about two hours north of the city. After college Randy would have been eligible for the draft and a free trip to Viet-nam, so he had a headhunter find him a teaching job, which would get him a draft deferment. He was hired as an English teacher at Monticello High School. The father of one of Ran-dy's students ran the Concord, so I got the job at the humon-gous hotel swimming pool, which was surrounded by nearly two thousand chaise lounges. The green midwestern WASP was off to the Borscht Belt.

I had heard of the area because of the famous pro basketball players who went up to the Catskills to play summer games at Kutsher's, and the many great fighters like Muhammad Ali who trained there. Three years earlier the epic Woodstock music festival had been held at Max Yasgur's farm about ten miles west of Monticello near the town of Bethel, which in Hebrew means "consecrated site." The grateful, stoned-dead attendees called the hospitable Yasgur "The Groovy Farmer."

I was oblivious to the importance of the historic little town of Woodstock sixty miles to the northeast, for which the festival was named. Woodstock was a well-known artists' community even before Bob Dylan ensconced himself there in the midsixties; it became a mecca for musicians such as The Band, Van Morrison, Jimi Hendrix, and Janis Joplin.

The Concord was the biggest Jewish hotel in the Borscht Belt. The *New York Times* called it "the gold standard of Catskills hotels." Thousands of Jews from the city vacationed in the Catskills. Many Jews came searching for a mate, or maybe just a one-night stand. There were over six hundred chaise lounges in the singles-only section at the pool, and everyone there was on the make. I was assigned a tame "family" section, away from the chaotic dating scene.

My name seemed to fit the place, but little else about me did. Many Jews coming to America over a century ago adopted Anglo-sounding names such as Sidney, Melvin, Milton, and mine, Sheldon. My mom just thought it sounded nice. When people at the Concord heard my name, they'd say, "Sheldon! You don't look Jewish!" Billy Crystal sullied the name in *When Harry Met Sally* when he told Meg Ryan that her former boyfriend Sheldon could not have been good in bed. "No one named Sheldon can be a great lover," he chortled. "A 'Sheldon' is your dentist or lawyer." Sheldon is the quintessential nerd, as in Alan Arkin's role in the movie *The In-Laws* or on the television hit *Big Bang Theory*.

On one of my first days in Monticello I was having breakfast at Charlou's Diner when a light-skinned Black kid sat down next to me. In a terrible stutter he asked, "Are y-y-you M-m-mister Anderson's b-b-b-brother?" I said yes, and he promptly informed me that he was the best player on the Monticello High School team. Randy had told him that a gunslinger from the Midwest was coming to town, so he challenged me to a game of one-on-one at high noon the next day. At least thirty Monticello High students skipped class to watch the big showdown between Chris "Wheat" Cummings and Mr. Anderson's brother. I won, but he was one of the best shooters I had ever played against. Chris and I became good friends and corresponded for years after. After playing junior college ball near Monticello, Chris played two years at Centenary College in Louisiana, a year after Boston Celtic great Robert Parish graduated. Chris did not feel at home in the Deep South: "Our coach is a hard core dude— much like a drill sergeant," he wrote me. "The social life here is not so cool. I still feel those racial tensions down here."

I eventually helped Chris get a basketball job in Bremerhaven, West Germany, where he, like Tom Norwood, has been ever since. He learned German, which he spoke without a stammer. I still have all of the newspaper clippings he sent me from high school, college, and Germany, most chronicling games in which he scored thirty or more points.

I played a lot of hoops that summer of 1972 because Hurricane Agnes hovered over Monticello for nearly a month. The rain kept the Concord's outdoor pool closed and the cabana boys out of work. On one of the few sunny days I went waterskiing with the Concord owner's sons, Richie and Steve White. My folks owned a lake cabin in northern Minnesota, so I was an excellent water-skier, but on one pass across the wake I fell head over heels on the slalom ski and knocked out three front teeth. Richie's uncle Marvin White had a dentistry practice in the Bronx, so I made several visits to see him. Marvin did me a huge mitzvah, charging me about forty-five bucks for a temporary bridge. Today that wouldn't get you past the receptionist.

On the Giants' trip to New York, I told Peter about the Concord, which had fifty tennis courts, three golf courses, outdoor basketball courts, two swimming pools, and nighttime live entertainment at the Imperial Room, featuring big acts such as Jan Murray, Jackie Mason, Judy Garland, Barbra Streisand, and Steve Lawrence and Eydie Gormé. I knew it would be a fun outing for the team, so we drove up from New York City and spent several days there. The team was overwhelmed by the enormity of the place, the excellent food, and the nightlife. They also liked watching boxers train for their next bout.

I'm sure that this was the first time that a big group of non-Jewish Germans had stayed at the Concord, although Marlene Dietrich had played the Imperial Room in the 1960s. I'm sure Dietrich did not bring along a German entourage, but then she was an American hero for refusing to work with the Nazi film industry. She stayed in Hollywood and became one of biggest stars on the U.S. military's wartime USO shows.

There had to be guests at the Concord who were Holocaust survivors or who had relatives who had perished in the genocide perpetrated by the Germans. For obvious reasons the Giants spoke German in low tones and kept a low profile, even my boss, Peter.

4

An American in East Germany

raveling behind the Iron Curtain on YMCA Hannover's road trip to West Berlin in 1977 whetted my appetite to revisit that foreign world of communist dictatorship and command economy. A year later another American player gave me the address of an elderly East German woman he had met on a train in West Germany. Liselore Detzer (née Schreiber) was on her way to see her cousin Rolf in Aachen, a German city on the Dutch-Belgian border.

The communists' supposedly progressive system could only be held together with political oppression, a ubiquitous secret police, and the Berlin Wall. Detzer lamented that her son and daughter were deprived of the opportunities to travel and experience the world outside of the Soviet bloc. Now, as a woman in her sixties, she was getting a chance to do that, and to bring back stories of life in West Germany and little treats like good chocolate and coffee. The East German ersatz versions were tasteless.

Detzer was able to travel to the Federal Republic of Germany (FRG), and I could get into East Germany, because of West German chancellor Willy Brandt's *Ostpolitik*—his "eastern policy"—launched in the early 1970s to pursue political, economic, and cultural engagement with the Soviet bloc. Brandt also sought to normalize relations with East Germany. After all, they were Germans, too, and still suffering from the aftermath of the war. East Germans had no political freedom and a much poorer standard of living than their countrymen to the west. Another rationale for *Ostpolitik* was to reach across the Berlin Wall to allow families and friends to reconnect. The German Democratic Republic began to allow pensioners like Detzer to travel to the West, not caring if they ever came back. Old folks were of no use to the communists; let West Germany pay their pensions.

The GDR got a good bargain with *Ostpolitik*. In return for loosening some restrictions on travel, the regime received de facto recognition from Bonn, economic assistance, and access to West German markets; in effect East Germany had an indirect connection through the FRG to the European Common Market. The autobahn from Hannover to Berlin had been built in the Nazi era, and became noticeably worse as one entered East Germany. A car had to slow down to absorb the pounding of the deep ruts between the forty-foot concrete slabs. With the border checks and the poor roadway, what should have been a two-hour trip from Hannover to Berlin lasted twice that. The East German government had no interest in devoting their scarce resources to facilitate more traffic from West Germany to West Berlin, so West Germany subsidized refurbishment of the highway. Bonn was also able to bargain away the machine guns on the border that were set to fire automatically on any East Germans trying to escape the workers' paradise. The East German government justified the border fortifications as a security measure to keep out West German spies and decadent capitalist influences, but they were in fact prison walls.

Detzer was born in Magdeburg in 1916, the same year as my mother. They were contemporaries in the "age of extremes," as historian Eric Hobsbawm called the twentieth century, during which humans killed each other on an unprecedented scale, spurred on by nationalist fervor and justified by radical ideologies on the communist left and the fascist right.

Three hundred years earlier was another age of extremes, when imperial forces of the Holy Roman Empire sacked Magdeburg during the Thirty Years' War (1618–48). In perhaps the most infamous battle of the war, the city was burned to the ground and some twenty thousand people were killed. One eyewitness left behind this record of the carnage, foreshadowing the wanton killing of civilians during World War II: "May God have mercy upon us henceforth, for this was a spectacle that has not seen its like in horror and cruelty in many hundred years, for it was beyond all measure. They [the imperial troops] drove small children into the fire like sheep, sticking them with spears; God knows Turks and barbarians would not have done otherwise."

Detzer's life is illustrative of the power of political and military leaders to determine the fate of ordinary people's lives. Political, constitutional, military, and diplomatic history is out of vogue in many history departments these days, sidelined by too many arcane cultural and social histories. It is one reason history departments have lost majors and faculty in recent years. Detzer lived through dramatic political upheavals far beyond her control, changes that affected her family in profound ways.

As a young child during World War I, Detzer was a subject of Kaiser Wilhelm II's Second Reich. When the kaiser abdicated and the Reich fell apart in 1918, she became a citizen of the newly formed Weimar Republic, the first truly democratic state in German history. Detzer lost her father in 1920; my mother lost her mother in the same year.

Detzer must have been affected by the deprivations suffered by the German people at the end of the war and by the hyperinflation in 1923, when the German currency became worthless, but she never spoke to me about her childhood or her parents. Parties on both the left and the right sought Weimar's destruction; the Depression further undermined Germans' support for that flawed democratic system. She was sixteen when Hitler and the Nazis took power in 1933. I asked her once about the Nazi regime. "I didn't pay any attention to politics, really," she said. I believed her. Maybe I wanted to.

Her cousin Rolf from Aachen *did* answer some of my questions about the Nazi period. He said that he was gratified by Hitler's defeat of France in 1940, in light of Germany's suffering, in his eyes, under the Treaty of Versailles. Luckily his family wound up in the American zone of occupation in Austria at the end of the war. He said that the American troops were "polite and helpful," except for the Jewish officers. "No wonder," he commented. Rolf repeated the old myth that President Roosevelt had sold half of Europe down the river: "The middle German—Russian zone—was a fatal gift from the sickly Roosevelt to Stalin [at Yalta]," he said.

There was no way for the western Allies to reverse the Red Army's gains in Central Europe at the end of the war. Some historians have argued that the western Allies should have leveraged their military position to the east of their assigned zones in May 1945 (including Detzer's Magdeburg) to extract political concessions from Stalin. That would have meant the end of Allied cooperation, however, and precluded Soviet entry into the war against Japan, which the United States badly wanted in early 1945. The atomic bomb had not yet been tested; in any case Washington had no idea if it would result in Japan's immediate surrender. An American breach of Allied agreements on the zones of occupation would have prompted Stalin to deny the western Allies their assigned sectors of Berlin, which was a far greater prize than Magdeburg. Magdeburg's fate was determined by the Red Army's presence in Central Europe, not by Roosevelt, who would have had to start a war with the Soviet Union to liberate the region from communist rule.

Befitting her maiden name, Schreiber (writer), Detzer wrote poetry and kept a thorough journal of her daily routine. She rarely commented on her own mental state in the journal, or analyzed the general political or economic situation in the country, although she did touch on her emotions in her poetry. She wrote about the destruction of Magdeburg in Allied bombing raids and the horrible suffering of the people. The city was an important port on the Elbe River, a railroad crossroads, the site of a Krupp steelworks, and airplane engine and explosive factories. The biggest raids came on January 21, 1944, and on January 16, 1945.

As the outcome of the war became clear in 1945, the Allies divided Germany into four zones of occupation. The eastern border of the Soviet zone ran to the west of Magdeburg, so after the Third Reich capitulated in May 1945, the U.S. Army withdrew into its assigned zone of occupation in the south of Germany. In effect the occupation lines agreed upon by Stalin, Roosevelt, and Churchill determined that Detzer would live in a communist dictatorship for the next forty years and that her cousin Rolf, who settled in Aachen, would enjoy the good life in democratic West Germany.

Detzer witnessed, in her words, the "proud and self-confident" American soldiers advance into Magdeburg in 1945; then she saw them leave and the Soviet Red Army move in. After the Nazis' total destruction of their country, and the loss of twenty-five million of their countrymen, the Red Army was bent on revenge. Some historians have estimated that Soviet occupiers raped a million German women, but who knows? One of Detzer's friends told me that the Soviet soldiers' behavior varied, but that freed forced laborers, mostly Poles, were on the rampage, looting and pillaging anything they could find. No wonder.

Liselore Schreiber met Kurt Detzer during the war. His son, Walter, had perished on the Eastern Front. Detzer's first wife was so despondent that she did not go into the cellar during a bombing raid on Magdeburg and died in the rubble. Liselore and Kurt married in 1946 and had two children, Walter (the second) and Lorelies. By the time I took my first trip to Magdeburg in 1979, Liselore had been a widow for nearly a decade.

The East German authorities allowed West Germans to get short-term visas to visit the GDR, most of them to see relatives. West Germans were understandably nervous about going inside the communist dictatorship. Who wanted to visit a strictly controlled police state that could arbitrarily detain you? With few exceptions, East Germans under the age of sixty-five could not get a visa to venture from behind the Iron Curtain.

The East German authorities discouraged tourism for fear of spies and personal contacts between its citizens and westerners, who might reveal to East Germans how much better life was in the West. They certainly didn't want Americans running around the country. On one trip to East Berlin I mistakenly exited the transit autobahn and was immediately pulled over by the East German highway patrol. They wanted to know if I was with the U.S. military in West Berlin. I told them I was a basketball player and they let me go.

A fabricated visa was the only way I could get into the GDR for a longer stay. A foreigner had to have an invitation from an East German, so Detzer claimed me as a long-lost relative, and I received a four-day permit to visit over the 1979 Christmas holiday. She put herself in jeopardy by lying to the authorities—it was a courageous thing to do. There was always the danger that her son and daughter would suffer the consequences of her liaison with an American. The state, after all, controlled all educational and occupational opportunities. Collective punishment of the families of politically unreliable citizens was a powerful means of thought control. I am sure that the Stasi—the East German security police—kept a file on Detzer and her American "cousin."

On the drive from Osnabrück to Magdeburg that Christmas, I had a lengthy delay on the East German border as guards combed through my BMW for contraband. The East Germans rolled a huge mirror on wheels underneath the car to make sure I had not stuffed a person into the undercarriage. I thought it strange that they thought that anyone would want to sneak *into* East Germany. Maybe they were just looking for banned items, but why would anyone think they could make money smuggling goods into a country devoid of hard currency?

The border guards also hassled me because I did not have Detzer's birthdate on my visa. They probably feared she was a young woman whom I had met in some other Soviet bloc country, and that the American was going to marry her and whisk a valuable worker off to the West. The guards also wanted to know how we were related. Detzer had told me that some distant relatives had emigrated to the United States in the nineteenth century, so I said she was a long-lost "aunt." I also had neglected to fill out a customs form and I didn't have a pen in the car, so I politely asked five or six East German guards for one. All of them turned me down. Finally a West German in line gave me something to write with, and I got through.

It was a gray, rainy day as I drove into the GDR, befitting my apprehensive mood. I was greeted with huge billboards celebrating the thirtieth anniversary of the founding of Germany's socialist state and its fellowship with the Soviet Union. That wasn't reassuring either. I didn't even have a map of Magdeburg, just Detzer's name and street address. At least ten passersby were of no help, so I drove to the train station, where I knew I could find a map, and located Sieverstorstrasse a few kilometers away. It took several more inquiries of passersby to send me in the right direction.

The layout of old European cities is a maze, so I took several wrong turns on the dimly lit and often unmarked streets. I noticed that some of the newer street signs honored the greats of the German communist movement, like Luxemburg, Liebknecht, Ulbricht, and, of course, Karl Marx. One sign of political revolution is the renaming of public places. Russia's St. Petersburg became Petrograd and then Leningrad during World War I; it is today back to the imperial St. Petersburg. In the Austro-Hungarian Empire, the Slovak capital of Bratislava today was Pressburg in German and Poszony in Hungarian.

The renaming of German cities, streets, plazas, and buildings, from those honoring the Kaiserreich to the Third Reich and the two postwar German states, mirror the radical political changes that the country underwent in the twentieth century. Obviously Göringstrassen and Hitlerplätze are no more. The new Marx-Engels signs in Magdeburg were not reassuring to this kid who grew up with streets named after Washington and Lincoln. Today the United States is undergoing some of the same reevaluation of the honorifics given to past political leaders and Confederate figures.

It was dark by the time I finally found Detzer's apartment building on 51 Sieverstorstrasse. I will never forget that address. There was a note on the door to knock; evidently the doorbell was kaput. There was no answer. So there I was in East Germany with no phone, no contacts, and nowhere to go. I thought I might have to turn around and drive right back out of the country. I imagined that the grumpy East German border guards would give me another grilling about my short stay.

Suddenly a plump, cheery, ruddy-faced woman came bounding up the stairs and threw her arms around me exclaiming, "Shel? Shel? You did come!" She kept rubbing her hands together, ecstatic that I had actually made the trip. She had been waiting for me at the train station, despondent that I had not arrived on the afternoon train from Hannover. I had written her that I would be driving to Magdeburg, which in German translates to "Ich fahre nach Magdeburg." The German verb *fahren* does not distinguish between driving by car or going by train. She could not imagine that I would drive a car to Magdeburg, let alone a BMW. A car was a luxury she had not even thought about.

Detzer's tiny two-room apartment was littered with the valuable old books she had saved from the bookstore that she and her husband owned until 1961. By then the communist state made it virtually impossible for private businesses to operate. Her shelves had books of every genre and in different languages. Detzer loved literature, which was her way to withdraw from the mundane, boring sameness of life in the GDR. I imagine that her books had also been a refuge from the Nazis and the horrors of the war. She was well versed in German literature; on that first visit we took a side trip from Halle to Weimar, not because of the city's political significance in the interwar period, but because it was the home of Goethe and Schiller, the great German writers of the late eighteenth and early nineteenth centuries. She and her daughter, Lori, recited their poetry, asking me if I knew any of it. When I said no, they asked me about great American poets like Emerson and Frost, but this philistine had committed nothing to memory.

The GDR, like every Soviet bloc country, was desperate for hard currency. Antiques, old books included, were one of few valuable items that the government prohibited East Germans from sending to the West. Nonetheless Detzer and her daughter gave me some old books that I managed to get through customs, such as Christoph Martin Wieland's *Oberon*, Friedrich Gottlieb Klopstock's odes, Christian Fürchtegott Gellert's fables (published in a series in the late 1820s), a tiny book of poems by Joseph Freiherr von Eichendorff, and a valuable 1825 edition of Goethe's *Faust*. Except for Goethe, I had never heard of the other authors.

We spent that first night exploring each other's strange worlds. Detzer knew nothing of basketball; what she knew about America came from her old books and West German television. Magdeburg was close enough to the border to pick up West German television signals, which East Germans were not supposed to watch. In that way the East German dictatorship mirrored the Third Reich; both regimes censored what their citizens could see and hear.

Detzer and I talked at length about my mother. Other than the Depression, my mother's traumas were personal, such as the death of her mother in the flu epidemic in 1920 and the gradual mental breakdown of her father, who was unemployed for most of the 1930s. Detzer's life course had been dramatically changed by events far beyond her inner circle. A year later I took Mom to East Berlin to meet her; despite the language barrier, they formed a close bond and corresponded for the rest of their lives.

Detzer and I also talked about religion. Although the communist authorities preached atheism and kept a watchful eye on the Evangelical and Catholic churches, she regularly went to church. Detzer was delighted to hear that my dad was a Lutheran minister, but I didn't tell her that I was a prodigal son. Wittenberg, where Luther posted his Ninety-Five Theses in 1517, is only about forty-five miles southeast of Magdeburg. She took me to the Magdeburger Dom, built in 1207, the first Gothic cathedral in German lands. Holy Roman emperor Otto the Great is interred there. The church converted to Protestantism in 1567, and was heavily damaged in World War II. None of the beautiful stained-glass windows survived, replaced by drab clear glass.

The next morning Detzer made a traditional German breakfast consisting of bread rolls, jam, cheese, sausages, and a soft-boiled egg. I had brought along some good coffee, which East Germans could not get. The German *Frühstück* is a leisurely way to start the day; one doesn't dawdle over a bowl of Wheaties. Detzer had sent me a letter asking what I liked to eat and drink; I wrote back something about juices. Fresh juices and citrus fruits were scarce in East Germany at the time, so she went to great lengths to find some ersatz juice concentrate. It was tasteless, but I drank it with gusto, knowing that she wanted to please her special guest.

The police state wanted to keep track of the American's whereabouts, so after breakfast we walked a kilometer to the precinct police station to register my arrival in Magdeburg. A few years later when I visited friends in Poland, I did not have to check in with the police. The authorities there didn't care, which is one of the reasons East Germany considered Poland to be an unreliable Warsaw Pact partner. The unity of the Warsaw Pact forces in defense of communism was a myth. National allegiance was a stronger pull than the unity of the working classes. The collapse of the communist states and the Warsaw Pact in 1989 is witness to that.

It was a typical north German winter morning—wet, cold, and oppressively gray. We passed by smoke-belching factories with big billboards featuring the "Worker of the Week." The air was saturated with the acrid odor of the low-grade brown coal that East Germans used to heat their homes. East Germany could not afford anything else; the environment was of no concern for a system that had to maximize production just to provide a minimal standard of living. After the Berlin Wall fell in 1989, the utter degradation of the land and water in East Germany was laid bare. The Federal Republic spent tens of billions of Euros to clean up the mess.

I will always associate that peculiar sulfur smell with the oppressive East German dictatorship. As we made the thirty-minute walk to the police station, I gripped my U.S. passport tightly as if it were my last link to freedom. At the station we were informed that we had to go downtown to register an American. I surmised that the local station did not have the means to get me into the surveillance system.

That afternoon we drove to Halle to spend Christmas Day with Detzer's daughter, Lorelies; her husband, Harald Hentze; and their two young daughters. Detzer said she had never dreamed that she would be chauffeured in such style. I put on some Christmas tunes and she fell deeper into reverie. "Shel," she sighed. "Du bist ein Glücksfall" (You are a stroke of luck).

Lorelies and Harald lived in a spacious second-floor apartment overlooking the Reileck, a busy Halle corner. I parked the BMW on the street below her apartment and we watched as it immediately became a source of great curiosity to passersby. A couple of days later while I was taking a jog around town—which proper Germans did not do because sport was to be done at a sports club—a couple of kids asked me if that was my BMW a mile away on Reileck.

The only passenger car that East Germany produced was the Trabant, a bare-bones, two-cylinder compact car with a fiberglass body. Like most consumer products made in the socialist countries, it was vastly inferior to western cars. It sounded like a lawn mower. Shortly after the Berlin Wall fell in 1989, Harald and Lorelies bought, as she put it, "a West car." Harald had a serious accident with that car; Lorelies said that if he had been in the flimsy Trabant he would have been killed.

For over thirty years the "Trabi" remained essentially the same. Without competition the state-run enterprise had little incentive to improve it. Nonetheless the Trabi was too expensive for the average East German. For those without connections—namely communist party members—there was a ten-year wait to get a new one. Nursing a Trabi into old age was an avocation for East German men, who had to know how to fix the simple machine.

When I saw people hovering around the BMW, I went down to the street and opened the hood. A gasp went up as the small crowd gawked at the car's complex innards. That engine was a blatant contradiction of communist propaganda about the GDR's workers' paradise. East Germans would have preferred to have been "exploited" workers in the capitalist West. It was the East German worker who was not getting the value of his labor. At least a West German laborer could buy a decent car, if not a BMW. Although it seemed that U.S. leaders were always fearful of losing the battle of Cold War ideologies, I never doubted that freedom, democracy, and the free market would prevail, especially after seeing up close the crummy products of the communist system.

Christmas at the Hentzes was warm, lively, and festive, but then Germans, like most Europeans for that matter, have made eating and drinking an art form. European waiters take their time to come around to your table; they don't bother you every five minutes with the obligatory, "Is everything okay here?"—which is really another way of telling you to hurry up so another party can use the table, making more money for the proprietor and more tips for the server. Car-crazy Americans invented the drive-in restaurant and then

10. My dear friend from the former East Germany—Liselore Detzer. A contemporary of my mother, Detzer was born during World War I, survived Allied bombing in World War II, and lived through five different German regimes. Courtesy of the author.

the even faster drive-thru fast-food joint. They snarf down their meal as soon as it hits the table, often in front of the TV. Too many Europeans have fallen into that rhythm, too. That's the downside of the competitive, dog-eat-dog free market.

The German Christmas is *gemütlich* unlike any other. That German word doesn't even have a direct English translation; it roughly means a romantic, cozy atmosphere. *Gemütlichkeit* elicits Rockwellian images of warmth, joy, and amity. Even on a cold December evening, the *Tannenbaum*, *Glühwein*, succulent bratwursts, and delicious sweets and pastries of the German *Weihnachtsmarkt* (Christmas market) warm the cockles. The Germans celebrate two days of Christmas, both punctuated by food, drink, and conversation. Although we had rabbit at the Hentzes, the traditional Christmas dinner is carp, which to a Minnesotan is a disgusting garbage fish. Smoked German carp, however, is quite tasty.

There was a special romance about Christmas in East Germany. Without the material abundance of the West, the holiday at the Hentzes was traditional and family-oriented. The Hentzes went to great lengths to decorate their apartment. Harald and his two daughters drove to a local forest to cut down a Christmas tree—illegally. Somehow they managed to elude the authorities as they hauled the huge tree back to their apartment.

Lori and Harald were disdainful of the communist regime. They had been approached by the secret police to spy on their neighbors, but declined. The Hentzes were probably under surveillance as a result. As protests against the regime escalated in 1989, they suspected that their telephone was tapped. The illegal tree-taking was a small act of defiance, and Harald wanted his children to be a part of it.

East Germans lived in fear of being fingered by the Stasi. On one trip to Halle I brought along another American basketball player. We were tossing around an American football when an elementary school teacher and her twenty students passed by the park. The kids were immediately curious about the odd-shaped ball and the tall guys throwing it. I told the students that we were Americans and threw the ball to them. The teacher curtly told her minions to end the conversation and moved them along with a furtive look back.

What most teachers would have considered a teaching moment she saw as a dangerous engagement with capitalists from the West. She probably feared for her job. The students' conversation with us was bound to get back to their parents, and from them to the authorities. If the communist dictatorship did not allow young people the freedom to travel, could not outfit them with blue jeans, forbade them to listen to rock 'n' roll or to watch western television, it was bound to fail. Lorelies told me that my visiting her high school English class was impossible.

After a lengthy continental breakfast we gathered again in late afternoon for "German coffee time" (with the coffee I had brought from West Germany). Lori began to cry. My visit, although welcome, reminded her of her French friend Martine, who had visited Halle a few years before. My coming brought home the fact that East Germans lived in a huge state prison; even right-wing authoritarian dictatorships allow their citizens to travel abroad. I tried to comfort her by saying that someday things would be different, but neither of us ever imagined that a decade later the Iron Curtain would fall. Her mother kept prodding me to tell stories about my many travels around the United States, but after Lori's breakdown that afternoon I didn't have the heart.

After dinner Harald took me to a local pub, much to the dismay of the ladies. The atmosphere was drab and the beer bad, but I think he was thrilled to have some male companionship. Harald is a free spirit, and he probably got vicarious pleasure from sitting with this strange American from the free world.

The Hentzes timed our long breakfasts, lunches, coffee times, and dinners by the candles on the Christmas tree, the light from which generated the *Gemütlichkeit* for our deep conversations. During the two hours that the candles burned we explored every aspect of the politics and economics of communism and capitalism. They were fascinated with America. They were all opposed to the GDR regime, but were not sure about the truth of their government's propaganda about the injustices of capitalism. A question that I heard over and over from people in the Soviet bloc was if one could buy this or that in the West, and how much it cost relative to an average income. They could not get over the easy availability of goods that were for them unattainable luxuries.

A parallel currency in communist countries was the time it took to find scarce consumer goods; once on a stroll through Halle I stopped to ask people standing in a long queue in front of a pet store what they were waiting for. "Fleas," they answered. "What? Fleas?" Then it occurred to me that the shop had not had fish food for a while, and they were desperate to keep their pet fish alive. People learned to jump into a line even if they didn't know what product was being sold. They could use it, trade it, or sell it on the black market. I caught on to that in my year living in communist Poland. If I stood in line long enough, I could score a decent bottle of Bulgarian red wine.

Women were the usual queuers. The communists crowed about their progressive, egalitarian policies toward women. The government needed women to work and provided free day care, but communist propaganda about gender equity rang hollow. Men held most of the important jobs in government and the economy. A woman has never led any communist country. Working women still did most of the traditional domestic chores. Husbands and fathers were not expected to cook, clean, and take care of the kids. I was always shocked when women from the Soviet bloc told me their age because they looked years older. Families were fortunate if they had retired grandparents to stand in line for them. A free market economy, despite its flaws, usually balances supply and demand.

These conversations with Detzer, the Hentzes, and other Germans were patently interesting, thoroughly informative, and highly stimulating. I had to concentrate to understand their stories and the nuances of their jokes in a foreign language. I had the same heightened sense of an attentive sponge during my stay in communist Poland several years later. Every synapse had to be firing. These were exciting adventures; I concede that as a result I have become a more impatient person today and am easily bored with idle conversation.

The next time I went to East Germany I met Detzer at her son Walter's house in East Berlin. Walter and his wife, Heidi, lived in a small two-bedroom house in Mahlsdorf on the eastern edge of the city. Westerners could cross into East Berlin on a day visa, but I had to be back at the border crossing before midnight to avoid being detained by the grouchy East German border guards. They were probably resentful of westerners' freedom to travel, as well as the nice cars that passed through Checkpoint Charlie. I made that trip to East Berlin many times, but on one trip I inadvertently left several West German newspapers on the floor of the car. I was hauled into the East German border station to answer questions about why I was bringing Western propaganda into the GDR. I explained that I had simply forgotten about the newspapers, and they let me go after an hour or so, with a stern warning never to do it again.

As I was appealing my case, I noticed the guards were detaining a Spanish kid for taking a wrong turn on the autobahn. He had driven all the way from Madrid to see a friend in West Berlin. On the East German autobahn on the outskirts of West Berlin, a sign directed drivers to "Berlin—Hauptstadt der DDR" (Berlin—capital of the GDR), or "Transit Berlin" to West Berlin. He had made the wrong turn to East Berlin and ended up there without a visa. He spoke no German and just a little English. I tried in vain to explain to the guards that he had made a simple mistake, which they obviously knew.

They curtly told me to mind my own business and sent me on my way. I have no idea how long they hassled the poor guy.

Walter Detzer was a high-school shop teacher, while Heidi worked for Mitropa, the catering service for the Reichsbahn, the East German railroad. The East German communist regime kept that incongruous name (meaning "empire railroad") for their railroad, because the GDR wanted to lay claim to the prewar railroad connections in West Berlin, and therefore make a legal claim to that part of the city. It was also cheaper to leave the old markers on the cars. The West German railroad was called the Bundesbahn (Federal Railroad).

Conversations with Heidi were contentious. Both Heidi and Walter had accommodated themselves to the East German system, she for ideological reasons and he out of resignation. Heidi's father was a leftist; she charged that Nazis and the businesses that had supported them had not been thoroughly purged in West Germany, as the communists had done in East Germany. This was indeed true, because as the western Allies began to fear the spread of communism in the late forties, they ended their denazification processes and enlisted West Germany as an ally against the Soviet bloc. For example, German expatriate Wernher von Braun was a key developer of the rockets that launched Apollo astronauts to the moon. During World War II he had helped the Nazis send v-2 rockets screaming terror and destruction into Britain.

Moscow had hauled off German scientists to work on Soviet space and weapons programs as well. And many former Nazi fellow travelers who ended up in East Germany were not punished as long as they pledged allegiance to the new communist state. It was a simple flip of the switch to take orders from a right-wing or left-wing dictatorship. Both systems promised security for those who went along (except for Jews and other "undesirables" in Nazi Germany, of course). Germans didn't have much experience with or devotion to democracy; even into the early 1950s a majority of West Germans were unsympathetic to the Federal Republic.

Heidi believed much of the regime's Marxist propaganda about the West—that big capitalists controlled all aspects of the government and economy; that workers and minorities faced relentless exploitation, poverty, homelessness, and discrimination; and that the western powers were imperialists bent on starting a war against the Soviet bloc countries. I disarmed her by admitting that some of what she said was true, and she had no answer for my questioning the lack of political freedom in the GDR. I could travel to East Germany or to any other country, but the Iron Curtain closed that opportunity for her. I reminded Heidi that the relative success of the East German economy and some of its infrastructure improvements were the direct result of huge West German subsidies. No other communist country received such largesse from the West. She also had no defense for the Berlin Wall. Over three hundred East Germans were fatally shot trying to cross the East German–West German border in the forty-year history of the GDR. No West Germans were killed trying to go in the other direction.

Heidi lauded the GDR for its egalitarianism, full employment, and cradle-to-grave social programs, including educational opportunities and health care for all. For East Germans who did not want the competitive stress of a free market economy, or who did not care about intellectual or physical freedom, communism provided a mundane, boring, yet predictable and safe life. Walter and Heidi could not lose their jobs and they had their basic needs met. They took advantage of the opportunity to travel cheaply to nearly all of the Soviet bloc countries, although it was a constant aggravation that, as East Germans, they could not stay in high-end hotels unless they had western hard currency. As long as one played along with the regime, however, life was low-risk.

I did see in Germans on both sides of the Wall a fear of instability and the breakdown of social norms. They really didn't mind taking orders, unlike those recalcitrant, individualistic Americans. I thought it odd to see a crowd of Germans standing at a red light without any cars in sight, with no one crossing until the light turned green. I got the stink eye if I walked on the red.

East Germans had an irrepressible urge for freedom, however; most of them were overjoyed by the fall of the Berlin Wall in 1989 and the incorporation of the GDR into the democratic Federal Republic in 1990. Committed communists and those who had accommodated themselves to the system were set adrift. Life in the unknown capitalist world would be hard for Walter and Heidi, as it was for the tens of thousands who lost their jobs, especially in the East German countryside. As Walter's sister, Lorelies, put it, after the GDR fell apart "we didn't know where we belonged."

5

From "Scheiss Preiss" to Bavaria

In 1980 I decided to leave one of the best basketball jobs in West Germany. I thought about making a life in Europe, but the inclement gray weather in Osnabrück was giving me the blues. It was always a surprise when the sun came out. I have no doubt that the northern Germans are more serious than their linguistic relatives to the south in part because of the cool, cloudy, wet weather. Who has ever heard of a German stand-up comic? Unlike the British, who suffer a similar climate, the Germans didn't have the ships or the empire to get away to warmer places and lighten their mood. And the Channel protected the English from the incessant fighting on the continent, from the devastating religious wars of the early seventeenth century to the Napoleonic Wars of the early nineteenth century, and then the horrors of trench warfare a hundred years later. Although eight hundred thousand British soldiers were lost in France in World War I, and British cities were smashed by German bombers in World War II, the battlefront never came to the British Isles. The last successful invasion of Britain came almost a millennium ago. Maybe there was time to laugh.

Peter was livid when I left his boys' club. I was, as the *Neue Osnabrücker Zeitung* put it, "the head of the team." My two years with the Giants were raucous fun, and I owe that to Peter, but he was not interested in building a successful long-term basketball program. He was kind of a poor man's George Steinbrenner, the former owner of the New York Yankees who gutted the farm system to acquire highly paid free agents. Peter never fully supported the club's youth teams, one of which I coached (both of his sons played for me). Another kid on my team was seven-footer Christian Welp, who went on to the University of Washington, winning two PAC-10 titles in the mideighties with fellow German Detlaf Schrempf. Both played in the NBA. Tragically, Welp died of heart failure in 2015 at the age of fifty-one.

Peter's stinginess with the lower-level club teams did not square with his spendthrift ways with the Giants, which made it to the top German league in 1983. The club's reputation as Peter's personal plaything eventually hurt attendance; the club's treasurer, Reinhard Niemann, had to make a plea for outside financial support. "We are not a club of millionaires," Niemann said, "but an entirely normal, common sport community that relies on ticket sales. . . . [We need a sold-out gym] to cover our costs." The fans knew that the Giants was anything but a normal club and that Peter was the man behind the curtain. They didn't respond to Niemann's plea and the team fell deeper into debt. Peter departed in 1984, and the infamous Giants finally fell apart in 1987, only a decade after its founding.

I decided to peddle my basketball skills and teaching credentials in Munich, the beautiful Bavarian capital near the Alps, just a few hours from Prague and Vienna, two of the magnificent cities of Cisleithania (present-day Austria) before the Hapsburg Empire collapsed in 1918. I wrote several letters to Munich teams inquiring about a basketball job. My German was pretty good by this time, but I started the letter with "Ich bin ein Amerikaner . . ." (I am an American). "Ich bin Amerikaner" is the correct German construction. President John F. Kennedy constructed a similar sentence in his speech in West Berlin in 1963. Kennedy's "Ich bin ein Berliner" can be translated as "I am a jelly doughnut," although most Germans did not take it that way. In northern Germany that confection is called a Berliner. In Minnesota it is known as a "Bismarck," after the Second Reich's famous chancellor.

It was a dumb way to introduce myself anyway, because anyone in West German basketball circles knew about the notorious Giants and its American player. The Deutsche Jugend Kraft (DJK) Sportbund München (German Youth Power Sport Association Munich) was the only club to respond. The DJK was a Catholic athletic association founded in 1920. After the Nazis came to power in 1933, the DJK was shuttered. In the so-called Night of the Long Knives on June 30, 1934, the Nazis murdered Catholic leaders, including Adalbert Probst, the head of the DJK.

The DJK came back after the war. The Munich club was headed by Helmut Handwerker, an erudite, unathletic, balding, middle-aged single man who lived with his mother. Handwerker was president of the Munich Sportbund for forty-seven years until his death in 2015 at the age of eighty-eight. He was an important figure in Munich basketball circles and a passionate supporter of the Sportbund, even to the point of making many enemies. One Munich newspaper called him both "respected" and "feared." He could be charming on the one hand and caustically judgmental on the other. He kidded me mercilessly about the "Ich bin *ein* Amerikaner" grammatical mistake.

Handwerker didn't play basketball, but he liked to take showers with the club teams. I thought nothing of it at the time, but some of the other players whispered about this peculiar behavior. It didn't dawn on me that Handwerker was probably gay, but he likely never acted on his impulses. Coming out as a homosexual in Germany at the time was a courageous act. Only a few decades before, the Nazis had arrested homosexuals and made them wear a pink triangle. That stigma didn't go away with the fall of the Third Reich.

Handwerker knew I was coming off a well-paying contract with the Giants, but I wrote him that I was not playing basketball in Germany just to make money. Handwerker offered me the use of one of the club's vans, a makeshift bedroom in one of the dingy offices of his used-book business, and help finding a teaching job at a Bavarian school. I took it.

Handwerker was intrigued by my interest in teaching and taking history courses at Munich's renowned Ludwig-Maximilians-Universität. The university is over five hundred years old, one of the oldest in Germany. What a thrill it would be to study where physicist Max Planck, novelist Thomas Mann, and Hans and Sophie Scholl—the martyred resisters to the Nazi regime—had walked the halls.

So I was off to Munich, a city that is linked to many ignominious twentieth-century historical events. I was twenty-nine when I moved to Munich in 1980; it was not lost on me that the Scholls were only a few years younger when they were guillotined in Munich's Stadelheim Prison in 1943.

Munich was the birthplace of the Nazi Party. Whenever I had a stein at one of Munich's famous beer halls, such as the Hofbräuhaus or Löwenbräukeller, I imagined Hitler in those cellars a half century before, haranguing the crowd about crimes of the Jews and communists, and the alleged injustices of the Treaty of Versailles. There must have been direct correlation between alcohol and Hitler's appeal to the losers who came to hear him. Walking by the Odeonsplatz I could almost hear the echo of the gunshots by Munich police that ended the Nazis' Beer Hall Putsch in 1923—Hitler's failed attempt to take over the Bavarian government and eventually the Weimar Republic. For that treasonous act he spent only nine months in prison. German authorities were less tolerant of prominent leftists: a few years earlier Rosa Luxemburg and Karl Liebknecht had been murdered in Berlin. Luxemburg's body was thrown into a canal.

Less than a mile away from the Odeonsplatz is the Führerbau on Arcisstrasse, where in 1938 Mussolini, Neville Chamberlain, and Édouard Daladier gave Hitler the green light to take the Czech Sudetenland. After they came to power in 1933, the first concentration camp the Nazis built was in Dachau, just a few miles outside of Munich.

A half century later, Munich's reputation was again sullied by the Black September terrorist attack on Israeli athletes at the 1972 Olympics. The West Germans wanted to use the Munich Olympic to erase memories of Hitler's highly successful 1936 Berlin Olympics and the crimes committed by Germans in World War II. A constant reminder of the war, however, was the hill on the site of the Munich Olympics, which was the now grass-covered rubble gathered from the bombed-out parts of the city.

The light, airy architecture of the Munich Olympic stadium stood in stark contrast to the powerful lines of the neoclassical Berlin Olympic stadium. Security forces at the Munich Olympics wore the light-blue colors of Bavaria, which were less intimidating than the black uniforms of the Nazis' ss or the brown shirts of the sa. Not wanting to invoke memories of the Nazi police state, security at the Olympics was lax, to say the least.

Occasionally I passed by 31 Connollystrasse in the Olympic Village, where the Palestinian terrorists took eleven Israeli hostages. The commandos had little trouble getting into the athletes' quarters; two Israelis were shot in their apartment and nine more perished in a botched rescue attempt at a Munich airport. I will never forget the words of ABC's Jim McKay when he got the tragic news about the hostages: "When I was a kid my father used to say, 'Our greatest hopes and our worst fears are seldom realized.' Our worst fears have been realized tonight. They're all gone."

The world today may have forgotten that brutal terrorist attack, but the anniversary is commemorated every year in Israel, contributing to the Israelis' belief that Palestinians were and are a dangerous threat to the Jewish state.

Munich also conjured up my memories of the controversial Soviet defeat of the U.S. basketball team at those same Olympics, the first time the United States had ever lost an Olympic basketball game. The gold-medal game was a tense, low-scoring affair; with ten seconds left the Soviets had the ball and a one-point lead. The U.S. winning streak seemed over until Illinois State University's Doug Collins stole a crosscourt pass and drove for the winning basket. The Soviet defender on the play, Zurab Sakandelidze, committed a foul that is considered the dirtiest play in basketball, and today would result in an automatic ejection. Sakandelidze undercut Collins as he tried to lay the ball in, flipping him over and driving his head into the stanchion. Woozy, Collins insisted on shooting the free throws. With three seconds left, Collins coolly sank both for a 50–49 lead, setting up a farcical finish.

The last three seconds were played three times. After Collins's first free throw the Soviets had asked the scorer's table for a time-out, which the referees did not recognize. The Soviets hurriedly inbounded the ball and dribbled up the court, but the officials stopped the game. The Americans wondered why the whistle had blown, but the scorer informed the referees that the Soviets had been requesting a time-out. The Soviets inbounded the ball again, and they missed a desperate shot from three-quarters court. The Americans danced around, ecstatic with their gold-medal win. But the scorer's table had failed to reset the clock to three seconds, so the court was cleared and the Soviets were given another chance. This time the Soviets lobbed a length-of-the-court pass to Alexander Belov, who nudged two American players out of the way, caught the ball, and laid it in for a Soviet victory, 51–50. The Soviets were delirious while the Americans stood in stunned disbelief. United States head coach Hank Iba was beside himself, running around from the referees to the scorer's table pleading for justice.

The Soviets were not complicit in some elaborate conspiracy to steal that game, but the bizarre ending fit into the American narrative of unscrupulous Reds who would use any devious tactic to win. There is some justification behind the three replays of the last three seconds. The U.S. Olympic

Committee filed a protest to the IOC, but to no avail. The Cold War enemy had beaten the United States at its own game. The American players refused to accept their silver medals, which remain unclaimed to this day.

Every week Sportbund practiced at the Rudi-Sedlmayer-Halle, where that gold medal basketball game was played. As I shot hoops there, I always wondered at which end of the court Belov had laid in the winning basket.

I have one other connection to the Munich Olympics. After losing my three front teeth in a waterskiing accident in the Catskills in 1972, I got a temporary bridge until I finished playing college ball. I took the bridge out for games, so I used to distract opposing free-throw shooters by showing my gap-toothed mug. My hockey-player kisser was not a pretty sight.

After college I got a permanent bridge, but in Munich I caught an elbow to the mouth, breaking off a piece of porcelain. Handwerker arranged for me to get a new bridge from the official dentist of the Munich Olympics. That forty-year-old bridge is still in my mouth—a constant reminder of Munich, that dentist, and the quality of German workmanship.

I had started my basketball career in West Germany playing for a Protestant club—the Hannover YMCA—and now I would be playing for a Catholic association in Munich. That made no difference to me, although as a kid I had the sense that Catholics were a strange lot. In Moorhead we lived just a few blocks from St. Joseph's, the Catholic school in town, but I had no connection to those kids. And when John F. Kennedy was elected in 1960—the first Catholic president in U.S. history—Dad commented, "Now the Pope will be running the country." I'm sure he later rued that statement.

Much to his credit Dad became *more* liberal and ecumenical in his old age, which is rare. Most people become more conservative and cranky as they get older. As Augsburg College president, Dad became good friends with St. Thomas College president Father Thomas Murphy. Alcohol can loosen up social discomforts, but I doubt that the Irish Catholic holy man from St. Paul and the teetotaler Norwegian Lutheran reverend from Minneapolis ever shared a beer.

These kinds of friendships make a huge difference in breaking down cultural barriers. Robert D. Putnam pointed out in his book *Bowling Alone: The Collapse and Renewal of American Community* that Americans have become more and more isolated from each other, as internet-surfing and TV viewing consume their leisure time. Information silos exacerbate people's animosities toward groups with a different ethnicity, class, and regional identity.

These days educators wring their hands about how to encourage diversity in schools and college campuses, as though putting people in the same room will automatically bring more interaction and understanding. Maybe team- and friendship-building through intramural and community sports would be a better method; basketball did that for me. A postgame beer with teammates from varied backgrounds might be the best sensitivity training there is. Studies show that those classroom training sessions are largely ineffective in changing people's attitudes. Go bowling together.

Over 150 years after the Civil War, the north-south cultural chasm in the United States remains deep. The northern border of Catholic Bavaria is also a Mason-Dixon line dividing northern and southern German traditions. The unity of the German people in one state is a historical anomaly. The Holy Roman Empire, which ended during the Napoleonic Wars, included most of the German-speaking areas of central Europe, but it was a decentralized system of kingdoms, princedoms, and duchies. After 1815 the German Confederation included thirty-nine separate polities, and the central government wielded little power. Protestant Prussia united most of the German-speaking regions in 1871; Bavaria was finally incorporated into a German state. Germany lost territory after World War I and was divided into two states after World War II.

Today there are still significant historical and cultural differences among the German states, which have considerable autonomy in the Federal Republic. The Protestant-Catholic divide in northern Germany is no longer very important (the rift between the former West and East German states is bigger now), but I soon learned that Catholic Bavaria is different.

Handwerker frequently wanted to know why I had wasted three years in the north—or "scheiss Preiss" (shitty Prussia in Bavarian slang), as he called it. It took me a while to understand the Bavarian dialect; the first time I went into a Munich bakery to get a *Berliner*, the woman behind the counter gave me a quizzical look. When I pointed to a jelly doughnut she said, "Oh, you mean a *Krapfen*."

Bavarian culture is like their big mugs of beer—lusty, happy, and frothy. Staid northern Germans are disdainful of Bavarian drinking habits. The northerners sip pilsners out of specially crafted brewery glasses with little matching doilies and coasters to catch the overflowing foam. It is supposed to take a barkeep seven minutes to pour a good pilsner. If you get your pils first, you have to wait patiently until your friends get theirs, otherwise you are obliged to buy the next round. In Bavaria, by contrast, the big steins of Oktoberfest beer come as fast as the dirndl-clad *Mädchen* can serve them.

I had worked as an English teacher at two public high schools in Hannover, so I thought I had a good shot at landing a job in Munich. I had one interview with a Munich high school, but unlike my job interviews in Hannover in which religion played no role, the Bavarians asked me if I was Catholic. The Lutheran did not get the job.

I seldom crossed paths with Americans in my three years of playing ball in Hannover and Osnabrück, cities that were in the British zone of occupation after the war. The Americans had wanted to occupy the north because this was the most important industrial area of Germany, but Churchill's arguments that Britain had suffered greater losses in the war and was geographically closer to northern Germany eventually carried the day. The United States took the southern zone, with the stipulation that the northern port of Bremer-haven would fall into American hands. The British got the unattractive but valuable Ruhr, but the Americans got fabulous vacation areas in the Alps and romantic cities such as Heidelberg and Munich. Shortly before I came to Germany, Hershel Lewis, against whom I had played my last college game, played with a team in Heidelberg.

Instead of working in a German school, I got a job as a substitute teacher at the Munich American High School, a U.S. Defense Department school for the children of servicemen, businesspeople, and diplomats. Most faculty members were middle-aged because Munich was one of the plum jobs in the system, and teachers with seniority wanted to teach there. They took a lot of sick leave, so I covered any subject and worked nearly every day of the week.

I played pickup ball that year with the servicemen at the U.S. Army base in Munich. Security in those days was shockingly lax, although terrorism was a threat in West Germany at the time. Since 9/11, U.S. military bases abroad have been guarded like Fort Knox. I simply drove my car onto the base, no questions asked. The most deadly terrorist organization at the time was the homegrown left-wing radical Baader-Meinhof Gang (a.k.a. Red Army Faction), which killed dozens of German businessmen and politicians in the seventies and eighties, and repeatedly targeted U.S. military bases. Because of the gang's penchant for stealing BMWs the car was jokingly called a Baader-Meinhof Wagen. Tragically, West German intelligence agencies were far more focused on the Red Army Faction's threat to the 1972 Munich Olympics than they were on a Palestinian terrorist attack on Israeli athletes.

The Bavarian authorities also missed terrorist threats from the extreme right. After World War II some twelve million Germans either fled or were kicked out of East Prussia, Poland, and Czechoslovakia. Many ended up in Bavaria, where they formed militant extremist groups, some aligned with neo-Nazis. The expellees were adamantly opposed to

Ostpolitik—the Social Democratic Party's policy to engage the Soviet bloc and recognize the postwar border changes—which meant the expellees' property claims in Eastern Europe would be null and void.

I was at the famous Munich Oktoberfest on the night of September 26, 1980, when a right-wing terrorist detonated a bomb, killing the bomber and twelve others, and injuring over two hundred. Several Sportbund players and I were a few hundred feet from where the bomb went off. The bomber, Gundolf Köhler, was a native German who had links to right-wing groups, and there is still some question today whether he acted alone. Some investigators thought it was an attempt to swing the upcoming national election toward conservative Franz Josef Strauss, the head of the Bavarian Christian Social Union. Right-wing groups in Germany accused the authorities of coddling the left and promised law and order. Nonetheless, Social Democrat Helmut Schmidt won the election.

Some of my best friends in Munich came from Czechoslovakia. They were not the Germans who were forced out of the Sudetenland at the end of World War II, but Czechs and Hungarians fleeing the country after the Prague Spring of 1968. The Warsaw Pact invasion of Czechoslovakia in August ended the communist party's attempt to liberalize the economy and allow greater freedom of expression. The suppression of this reform movement, dubbed "Socialism with a Human Face," was the death knell of Soviet-Marxist ideology. The communist dictatorships, some calling themselves "people's republics," could only survive if tanks crushed the people's voices.

My coach at Sportbund was Franz Losonsky, a swarthy, mustachioed, jet-black-haired Hungarian from Czechoslovakia. After the collapse of the Austro-Hungarian Empire at the end of World War I, Hungary was left with a rump state, losing two-thirds of its territory and a third of its population. Hungarians ended up in Romania, Yugoslavia, and Czechoslovakia (the vast majority in the Slovakian half of the country). To this day some two million Hungarians still live outside of Hungary.

Losonsky fled Czechoslovakia after the Prague Spring. He recruited our center, Czaba Ferenczy, a fellow Hungarian. I also became a close friend of Renata Kronberger, a player on the German women's national team. She was Czech by birth, having left Czechoslovakia as a young girl with her parents in 1968. Their stories, along with the experiences of my friends in East Germany, piqued my interest in pursuing graduate studies in central European history.

In my four seasons of basketball in West Germany, I had always kept graduate school in my sights. I padded my grad school resume by taking history courses at the University of Minnesota every summer after the German basketball season was over. I used German-language sources for several term papers, which probably impressed the professors in the Minnesota history department.

I also took history courses in Osnabrück, Münster, and Munich. West German universities kept a certain number of spots open for foreign students. Law and medical studies were more sought after than history, so I had no problem matriculating. Germans who had completed their high school Abitur went to the university virtually tuition-free; I got that deal, too.

The German student's life was good, albeit modest. Many became "professional students," working odd jobs here and there, hanging out in coffee houses and dive bars, and enjoying the university's cheap room and board. Some stayed in school for a decade. Students had few obligations to attend classes. Seminar attendance was mandatory, but otherwise students just had to pass exams in their majors every six months or so. In recent years many European universities have instituted modest fees to discourage the lingering scholars.

I was fortunate to take courses from two eminent German historians, Klaus Hildebrand at the Westfälische Wilhelm-Universität in Münster, and Dr. Thomas Nipperdey at Ludwig-

Maximilians-Universität in Munich. The Westfälische university is named for Wilhelm II, the last German kaiser. Hildebrand was a prolific author of books on the Kaiserreich and Third Reich foreign policy. Twice a week I drove the forty-five kilometers from Osnabrück to Münster to hear him lecture.

Good pedagogy was not high on the priority list of German history professors in those days. Many treated teaching as a job obligation that got in the way of their research. Unfortunately teaching undergraduates is no longer the top priority at many American universities either; professors are awarded tenure and promotion on their publication records even if they are mediocre, indifferent teachers.

There was also a deep divide between the esteemed German professor and the lowly student. Hildebrand's lecture class fell apart one day in a clash between the arrogant, stiff, Prussian-like "Herr Professor Doktor" and a cell of Marxist students. Those comrades were inspired by the ideological zeal of their forebears in the German leftist movement, which Hitler had obliterated in the 1930s. In the late sixties West Germany was experiencing a generational clash that hit most of Western Europe and the United States. The focus of revolt in America was civil rights, women's liberation, and the Vietnam War, while West Germany's strife centered on class struggle and the contested memory of Hitler's crimes. The older German generation naturally wanted to forget the shame of the Third Reich; they were resistant to dredging up the recent past and coming clean about their role in it. West German secondary school teachers at the time often passed over the Nazi period for fear that the subject would open up painful intergenerational inquisitions.

When I was teaching in Luxembourg in 1993 and playing ball with a club across the Moselle River in Trier, I asked several of my young German teammates about Hitler's *Anschluss* (annexation) of Austria in 1938, which was the subject of my lecture the next day. None of them had any idea what *Anschluss* meant in the context of German history. I asked them if they had had any instruction in the history of the Third Reich; they said that their history lessons had started with the Greeks and Romans and that their teachers never made it to the twentieth century. I told them that I thought German history lessons should *start* with Germany's attack on Belgium in 1914 to begin World War I, and then deal with the Nazi period in depth.

This was a small sample of students, of course. Some German states mandated curricula on the Nazi era. Today most German students get a thorough briefing on that most difficult and shameful period of their history.

The East German communists dealt with the subject of German guilt by blaming the capitalist class, which the East German leadership claimed they had eradicated by nationalizing the economy. The East German leaders portrayed Hitler as a lackey of big business and Nazism as a last gasp of the ruling classes to hang onto power before the inevitable victory of the proletariat. Leftists saw continuity between the dominance of big capital in the Third Reich and that in the Federal Republic. The East Germans' analysis of the rise of the Third Reich was more propaganda than good history. The communists lacked popular support, so they welcomed Nazi Party converts, many of whom easily transitioned to the GDR dictatorship by dutifully obeying their new Marxist marching orders.

West German Marxists echoed East German critiques of capitalists and their support of the Nazis, and the fact that West Germany had not purged former Party members from their free market economy. They pointed to the many big businesses, such as Bayer, Siemens, and Volkswagen, that had flourished in the Third Reich and were still thriving in the FRG. That was the rationale for the Red Army Faction's kidnappings and murders, which often targeted men who had served the Nazi regime.

Hildebrand downplayed Hitler's support from the social and economic elites, arguing that Hitler's personal philosophy and idiosyncratic foreign policy goals had played a major role in the rise and fall of the Third Reich. Hildebrand rejected the *Sonderweg* (special path) theory of militaristic, authoritarian, and anti-Semitic German history that had put the country on the inevitable path toward Nazism.

Leftists criticized Hildebrand's "intentionalist" focus on Hitler's dominant role in the Holocaust. Hildebrand deemphasized a Marxist interpretation that stressed the class character of Hitler's rise to power in 1933. "Hitler's programmatic ideas about the destruction of the Jews and racial domination," Hildebrand wrote, "have still to be rated as primary and causative, as motive and aim, as intention and goal of the 'Jewish policy' of the Third Reich."

During one of Hildebrand's lectures on Nazi foreign policy, several Marxists in the upper rows of the hall shouted, "Dr. Hildebrand, we have a few questions about your interpretation of the rise of Nazism." Hardly looking up from his lectern, Hildebrand responded, "I do not answer questions during my lecture." The students persisted; Hildebrand repeated that he would not answer them. After the students yelled at him a third time, he packed up his notes into his briefcase and stalked out. That was that. On the one hand I thought the episode was amusing, but on the other my hour-and-a-half drive to and from Münster had been a waste of time.

I had to admire the passion of those students. I wish I had the same engagement from my students today, some of whom tell me that they do not like to talk about politics. Sometimes for laughs I ask my diplomatic history class if there are any Marxists among them; they just smirk. Not that I want them to be Reds, but in thirty years I've had only one or two raise their hand.

Nipperdey taught modern German history at Ludwig-Maximilians-Universität. His many books and articles are still required reading for scholars in the field. Shortly before his death in 1992 Nipperdey completed his masterpiece, a massive three-volume history of Germany from the Napoleonic era to the end of the Second Reich in 1918. In Nipperdey's obituary in the journal *German History*, London School of Economics history professor John Breuilly wrote, "Nipperdey was one of the most outstanding and significant historians of his generation. . . . He had that rare capacity to cast a fresh light upon a subject in a short compass, stimulating others to explore those ideas in greater depth."

Nipperdey's lectures on German history were masterful, but apparently my fellow students at Ludwig-Maximilian were not so moved. About fifty students showed up for Nipperdey's first class, but when they found out that the lectures came directly from his books they stopped coming. By the second week fewer than ten of us were showing up, but Nipperdey rambled on as though the lecture hall were full.

Sportbund had a winning record that year. Even though he had a hard time admitting it, Handwerker was happy with our performance. He wanted me back for another year, but without a permanent teaching job I decided to pursue a PhD in history at the University of Minnesota.

In 1981 a Bremerhaven newspaper announced my departure from Europe, calling me a "model sportsman." Yakovos Bilek, the head coach of the German national basketball team, said that "Sheldon Anderson is the most intelligent point guard that I ever saw play in Germany." I was not a pure point guard, but I'll take "model sportsman" and "most intelligent." That high praise probably stemmed from my fluency in German, immersion in German culture, and focus on studying European history, which were unusual for an American basketball player. And I vaguely recall that the reporter was an acquaintance.

In the fall of 1981 I began graduate school at Minnesota. I assumed that my professional basketball career was over, but soon I was flying back and forth from Minneapolis to play in European Cup games for the Osnabrück Giants. Six years later I used a basketball connection in communist Poland to finish my PhD dissertation research.

6

Wild Turkeys, WACers, and Southside Johnnies

I used to kid Fitz, my old basketball rival from St. Thomas College, about his tight-knit circle of Irish Catholic friends in St. Paul. As the crow flies, the Fitzpatrick house was less than a mile east of the Andersons' on West River Road in Minneapolis. Fitz never ventured across the Mississippi River and I never went his way either. He went to grade school and college in his neighborhood, then bought a house right across from St. Thomas. Fitz didn't own a car until he was in his midtwenties.

Except for my five-year foray into German and Polish basketball, I was equally insular. I was born at the now-shuttered Lutheran Deaconess Hospital near Bloomington and Franklin Avenues, which is a short stroll from my high school, college, and graduate school. The University of Minnesota straddles the Mississippi, and the West Bank of the university is right across Riverside Avenue from Augsburg College.

During graduate school at Minnesota in the 1980s, I lived in an ugly high-rise apartment building in the West Bank Cedar-Riverside neighborhood. It reminded me of the drab, boxy, cookie-cutter apartment complexes in East Germany. The Cedar-Riverside builders decided to put blue and red panels on the gray cement facade, which was, as the saying goes, like putting lipstick on a pig. The panels were just more eyesore.

When I was playing ball in Europe people used to ask me what Americans were like. "Which ones?" I replied. "New Yorkers or Alabamans? Floridians or Californians? New

Orleanians or Minneapolitans?" Unlike New Orleans, Minneapolis's cool jazzy Mississippi River neighbor to the far south, the lily-white Mill City never had much of a reputation for music and nightlife until the Cedar-Riverside scene hit in the sixties, and again when Minneapolis native Prince splashed onto the stage in the eighties. In 1884 the Minneapolis City Council limited saloons to downtown, riverfront areas and a few nearby residential areas, all of which could be patrolled at night by cops on horses. Cedar-Riverside was one of those areas, but bars still had to close at 1 a.m. After Prohibition ended in 1933, 3.2 beer joints still flourished in those neighborhoods. You still can't buy beer or wine in Minnesota grocery stores, but you can get the watered-down brew.

The Big Easy's music scene need not have feared competition from the West Bank, but Cedar-Riverside became Minneapolis's version of Haight-Ashbury, home to honky-tonks, cheap ethnic eateries, and dive bars. It was safe, cheap, and countercultural. The Triangle Bar on Riverside, built at the turn of the century, was a two-story miniature of New York City's famous Flatiron Building, which was erected several years later. The Triangle was a hopping venue for the likes of Willie and the Bumblebees, and "Spider" John Koerner. When the Bees' sexy sax player Maurice Jacox jumped up on the bar "The Angle" went nuts. "The Triangle draws West Bank freaks, spooky people with dark glasses, cowboy hats, patched jeans, leather jackets," wrote one journalist. "It's so crowded that at times you can only stand there and watch a musician rub his belly, groping for the microphone: 'Testicles, 1, 2, 3.' The bands at the Triangle seem devoted to making as much noise as they can—it spills out the door and keeps the whole West Bank awake till 1 a.m."

My high-rise apartment building was part of a sad story of slash-and-burn development projects and failed social engineering in the 1960s. Minneapolis was not alone among U.S. cities that destroyed beautiful old buildings such as the Great Northern Station and the magnificent Metropolitan

Building in the downtown Gateway District, which was the biggest historic architectural loss. Fortunately, the thirty-two-story Foshay Tower, modeled after the Washington Monument, did not meet the wrecking ball. In 1971 city planners allowed Kmart to build on Lake Street, smack-dab in the middle of Nicollet Avenue, cutting off one of the city's most important north-south arteries.

Well-meaning sociologists and urban planners wanted to create a "new town in town" in Cedar-Riverside, which was a haven to hippies who lived in the run-down tenement walk-ups. Developers decided to build several high-rise buildings for lower-, middle-, and higher-income tenants, make money on that, and then tear down the tenements for retail shops. The West Bankers liked their old town in town and balked at living in a multistory box of reinforced concrete, which someone dubbed "The Ghetto in the Sky."

Ironically the eggheads' utopian socialist theory jibed with the tie-dye set's inclusive weltanschauung, but not when it came to reality. The sociologists' hope that the rich would rub shoulders with dope-smokers and flower children in an ugly skyscraper was pure fantasy. To scrimp on costs, the developers installed only three elevators for the tallest building, thirty-nine stories high, so the wait for an elevator could be five to ten minutes. Good luck in getting the mucky-mucks to live in a penthouse that they couldn't get to. There were no service elevators, so moving in or out of an apartment had to be done in the dead of night. It came as no surprise that after several years the high-rises were in receivership. My seventy-buck-a-month, nineteenth-story, HUD-subsidized studio apartment was spare, but I had a beautiful view of the West Bank.

A lot of West German friends came to stay with me in my cramped little abode. Cooped up in an overpopulated country that was little bigger than Minnesota, many of them wanted me to help them buy a car to drive westward to the Pacific so that they could indulge their wanderlust for *Lebensraum*.

Eventually I had to limit the number of visitors because the Germans—as they are wont to do—tended to occupy my one room longer than they were welcome.

Whether from behind the teacher's desk or in front of it, I have spent most of my life in the classroom, so it was a smooth transition from playing hoops in West Germany to starting my PhD program at Minnesota. I love the rhythm of the school year and the feeling of accomplishment at the end of the semester when grades are meted out. I can't imagine working a nine-to-five in the beautiful Minnesota summer, when Minnesotans are busting out of their sixth-month hibernation. And, of course, there is always time for ball games.

Studying and teaching by day and playing games by night has been my healthy routine for over six decades. My brother, Randy, was in a master's program in American studies at the time I was playing ball in Germany, so while I was taking courses at Minnesota during the summer, I played on his intramural coed slow-pitch softball team. Aside from Randy, the American studies roster was full of eccentric academics with few softball skills. Our pitcher was rotund Robert, whose first job out of grad school was peddling penis pumps to impotent men. Bob's biggest fear was getting hit on a hard comebacker because he could not get out of the way. We called ourselves the "Wild Turkeys" because Bob got us free T-shirts from the distillery where I think he had done research for his master's thesis. It was a funny name for our team, but not as clever as that of our rivals from the psychology department, the "Nocturnal Emissions."

The Wild Turkeys had a logjam at catcher because it is a meaningless defensive position in slow-pitch softball, which does not allow stealing bases. Laura and Diane shared the "catching" duties. Most of the time they stood by the backstop and fetched the ball after it had stopped rolling. Their errant throws back to big Bob brought the game to a crawl. Laura and Diane's fielding skills might have inspired the old joke, "What do that fielder and Michael Jackson have in common? They both wear a glove for no apparent reason."

We called Laura "Scarlett" because we didn't know any other southern women. She had a beautiful drawl and all of the southern belle stereotypes. Scarlett loved her hunky men. Her pugnacious little Dixie boyfriend, Terry, was in the American studies program, too; despite his diminutive stature he tried to hit every pitch out of the park, only to fly out every time (the fields had no fences, so outfielders could play deep). But he wanted to impress his lady, so he kept trying to go yard, much to the chagrin of Randy and me. With seven-inning games, our motto was don't make one of those precious twenty-one outs.

Scarlett eventually dumped Terry for Randy's college roommate, Paul the Wall, a ringer on our team who actually *could* hit home runs. He got his nickname because he didn't say much. Back then we gave nicknames to everyone. Today people are overly sensitive about these kinds of monikers, but for us they were terms of endearment. Paul the Wall evolved into "Wally Tater" (tater is slang for a home run, and Wally Gator was a Hanna-Barbera cartoon character). Wally Tater was silent and big, just how Scarlett liked it. But like Terry and his long fly-outs, Wally drove Randy and me nuts because on an extra-base hit to the outfield gap he would just heave the ball back into the infield as far as he could, just to show off his arm, but missing the cutoff every time.

Scarlett ended up running a law firm and married The Wall, but to no one's surprise they divorced after a couple of years. They had no kids, but when Scarlett skipped town she left him with her two enormous Weimaraners. At least The Wall had someone to talk to.

Diane, like many American studies majors, wanted to become the next great American novelist. Her dad owned a big hotel in Wisconsin, but her parents had divorced when she was a little girl. That probably made a lasting impression on her, for she was unhappy in love and life. After finishing her degree, she changed her name and wrote a short memoir and a coffee-table book on country-and-western fashion. Diane's boyfriend, Peter, was fast on the bases, but rarely got there because he had trouble connecting with a slow-pitched softball. Peter ended up in Chicago shilling Mars candy bars for a big advertising firm.

Of all of the Wild Turkeys from that American studies cohort, Randy became the most successful writer. During graduate school he edited the music section of the *Minnesota Daily*, one of the top university newspapers at the time, and from there became chief editor of *City Pages*, a local weekly newspaper. Then he started a successful small company writing speeches, scripts for annual business meetings, and other commercial literature. I used to kid him about wearing sweat pants to work at *City Pages* and then donning Brooks Brothers suits for the corporate crowd.

Writing in suits for suits became a bore, so Randy moved to Los Angeles to work in movies and television. How many writers and actors have gone to Hollywood with that dream? But to his credit he perfected his craft and landed on several television shows, writing for such critically acclaimed shows as *Homicide*, *Chicago Hope*, and *The Fugitive*.

Gary was the only other Wild Turkey to go on for a PhD, and he could actually play a little ball. He got the handle "Scratch" by entering the long jump at the university intramural track-and-field meet and scratching all three times. He ended his university track-and-field career without ever posting a legal jump.

Scratch wallowed in that kind of self-deprecation. Years before he had thrown out his rotator cuff on his throwing shoulder, but he wanted to play third base anyway, which is the longest throw in the infield. Scratch had to swing his body around like a rusty gate to get his stiff, arthritic arm to follow.

During my summer-school semesters at Minnesota, Scratch and I would meet at the library around midnight

BIG LEAGUE CARDS ®

GARY O. 'DOC' LARSON
OAKLAND Z's   1985

11. Gary "Scratch" Larson wearing the colors of his beloved Oakland A's and San Francisco Giants. He got the moniker "Scratch" *after* this photo was taken. I am indebted to Scratch for putting me up at his tiny studio apartment (The Foggy Bottom Institute—FBI) when I did research at the National Archives for my first two books. Courtesy of the author.

for a couple of hours of study. Scratch had his idiosyncratic routines that never changed, kind of like Dustin Hoffman's autistic Raymond in *Rain Man* ("Wopner at Five"). Scratch made a cheese sandwich for lunch every day, along with some carrots or another cold veggie. He watched reruns of *The Rockford Files* at 10:30 every weeknight and then headed off to the library. Scratch always sat in the fiction section; if he got some solid work done on his dissertation, he would pull a Dashiell Hammett or Raymond Chandler mystery novel that he was reading off the shelf and treat himself to a chapter.

One of Scratch's favorite Minneapolis diners was The House of Breakfast. The minimalist joint didn't have a menu, just paper plates tacked on the wall with the various offerings written on them. One simply read, "Pancake." Scratch liked to eat at greasy spoons that had just reopened after getting closed by the health department because he figured that the place would be spankin' clean, for a little while anyway.

Scratch grew up in Oakland and is still an inveterate fan of *any* Bay Area team, from the 49ers to the Cal Bears. But baseball is his first love. Scratch had a cap with a bill front and back; an Oakland A's emblem was on one end and a San Francisco Giants logo on the other. He used to call his mom late at night for the ninth inning of a Giants or A's game, and have her hold the telephone close to the radio so he could listen to the last inning. Scratch still doesn't have cable television, but he lives in the Bay Area now so he can tune into the games without bugging his mom.

After finishing his PhD, Scratch went to work for the National Endowment for the Arts (NEA) in Washington DC. He drove his beat-up old forest-green Volkswagen Beetle from Minneapolis to Washington, packed full of books and a few clothes. The driver's seat on the car had rusted up in its most forward position so that Scratch's chest was inches away from the steering wheel and his head right up against the windshield. It looked like the "jaws of life" would have to extract him, accident or not.

Scratch is a huge fan of jazz greats such as Mingus, Monk, and Coltrane. He even named his son Miles after Miles Davis. Scratch is a superb jazz pianist, but he rarely played for the public. When I stayed at Scratch's place on K Street, he would switch on his electric keyboard's built-in drum machine, put on his headphones, and bang away without a sound going anywhere but into his own head. Occasionally I got him to play for me. I don't know jazz, but I knew that he was good. I told him he should share his talent with others. He did do a gig or two at a bistro up the street, but that was it. Scratch played music for his own pleasure. Maybe that's the definition of a pure artist—the painters, sculptors, and writers who produce for themselves without trying to please the public.

I owe a big debt of gratitude to Scratch, who always shared his tiny studio apartment in Foggy Bottom during my many research trips to the National Archives. He called it the FBI—the Foggy Bottom Institute. Scratch's office with the NEA was in the Old Post Office, which is now the Trump Hotel. Scratch and I would take the Metro together to Federal Triangle stop. He loved showing me his absolute mastery of the DC subway system, right down to his deft insertion of his train ticket into the turnstile so he could walk right through without hesitation. I practiced his technique; eventually we would race to see who could get through the turnstile first. It was a stupid little game, but it was one of those quirky little parts of Scratch's day that brought some fun into an otherwise mundane routine.

Scratch and I walked through a gauntlet of panhandlers at our Foggy Bottom Metro stop. Most people feel a little guilty about ignoring beggars, but Scratch had a rule. If one of them said, "God bless you," "Go Giants," or, "Go A's" (responding to either end of his cap), Scratch would stop and give him some change. It was a "pay for work" kind of thing.

The last time I stayed with Scratch in the late nineties he had packed up all of his books for a move back to his beloved Bay Area. They were stacked so high against the walls of the

FBI that some were leaning precariously. I actually thought they would come crashing down on me during the night. I imagined this headline: "Cascade of Books Crushes Professor in Foggy Bottom."

Years later I attended an academic conference in Berkeley, not far from where Scratch, his wife, Bettina, and Miles live. He insisted on picking me up at the San Francisco airport, which is a long drive from Oakland. I expected to meet them curbside, but Scratch parked the car so the family could meet me inside the airport. It took Scratch a half hour to find the car again; he did better with mass transit.

In my first couple of semesters at Minnesota I was still playing basketball in Europe. The Osnabrück Giants flew me back to Germany to play in European Cup games. The German league allowed one foreigner, but the European Cup tournament permitted two. Arnette Hallman from Purdue was the Giants' American, and I was the "Non-stop Flyer [*Dauerflieger*] as Secret Weapon," as the *Neue Osnabrücker Zeitung* put it. It was an exhausting routine, but for an impoverished grad student it was a lucrative deal. My colleagues thought I was nuts, but I had no trouble balancing my studies and the travel because I took my reading with me on the plane. Eight hours thirty thousand feet in the air made for valuable reading time. In those days there were no distracting movies or internet.

I last played for the Giants in the fall of 1983, beating Iraklis Saloniki in a European Cup game. A few months later Hallman abruptly refused to play because of a contract dispute with Peter. I was asked to come over to play a couple of league games. At first I agreed and the flight was booked, but when I found out that Hallman had left the team, I declined. "Anderson: Erst ja—dann nein [first yes and then no]," the *Neue Osnabrücker Zeitung* reported. "The Giants' key player for many years . . . didn't want to stab Hallman in the back."

When I began grad school in 1981, Randy and I organized the next iteration of our university intramural softball team, the WACers (hard *C*). The Wednesday Athletic Club (WAC) began in Monticello, New York, half a century ago. After Randy finished his undergrad degree at Minnesota in 1969, he took an English teaching job at Monticello High School to get a deferment from the draft. Teachers did not have to go to Vietnam. Every Wednesday night the Monticello teachers went to Rourk's Tavern for a round of beers and a game of feathers (darts).

This WAC tradition migrated with Randy back to Minnesota when he began work on his master's, and from there to my job at Miami University in Oxford, Ohio. The WAC has long since lost any connection to Wednesday or athletics—as if one can call darts a sport—and it has always been open to men, women, athletes, non-athletes, and any other rounders with a sense of humor. When I played ball in Poland in 1987, I wore a WAC T-shirt—with the tilted drunken W—for a photo and interview that appeared in the newspaper *Kurier Lubelski* (Lublin Courier).

One of the first new WACers at Miami University was a guy I called "Ice," who became my best friend in the history department. Years later I found out (not from him) that I was not his top pick for the job. I thought that was really funny. Ice is a brilliant scholar and writer, having published several highly regarded monographs. He did a biography of gangster John Dillinger, joking that he was intrigued by Dillinger's legendary appendage.

I gave him the nickname Ice not because he is in any way cool. He and I lived in Cincinnati, so we car-pooled up to Oxford, which is about forty-five miles north. When it was his turn to drive and there was *any* hint of sleet or snow on the road, he'd panic and hand his keys over to me. Ice was from Los Angeles and figured the kid from Minnesota could handle it.

Ice fashions himself as a lovable loser, a nebbish like Woody Allen's Fielding Mellish in *Bananas*. His favorite line is "I got nuttin." I thought Ice was a little nutty, but I was surprised to learn that he went to a shrink. I asked him once if he thought he was getting cured. "I'm in analysis," he snapped, "not therapy." I told him that Norwegian psychoanalysts just tell patients to hold everything in and not to bother anyone with their problems. Go fishing.

When I met first Ice in 1991, he was going through a tough divorce, like several other middle-aged male colleagues in the department. In the old days college faculties were predominantly male; they dragged their wives to whatever teaching job they could find. Miami (not Florida) University in Oxford (not England) was probably not a wife's first choice of a place to live for the rest of her life. After the kids had grown up and left Oxford, many wives realized just how unhappy and unfulfilled they were in that small college town.

On the night that Ice signed his divorce papers, Art, his best buddy from the English department, suggested that we usher Ice back into the singles' world by taking a road trip to the "Hitching Post" in Darrtown, Ohio, a widening in the road about five miles from Oxford. Famed Los Angeles Dodger manager Walter Alston grew up there and went to Miami University. Our history department colleague Jack joined us for the sad affair, not because there was going to be any hitching going on but to commiserate; he had gone through his own divorce a few years earlier. Wild Turkey was Jack's drink of choice; he kept a bottle in his office desk. Whenever Jack had a couple of belts he would regale us with his research on the environmental history of North Carolina or some other such esoteric, erudite subject until we, too, begged for a drink. We loved Jack, rest his soul.

Ice rarely drank much, but he had a few Turkeys that night. Back in Oxford we dragged him into DiPaolo's for a nightcap. Art kept calling for more rounds and had the proprietor bring Ice a restaurant T-shirt to commemorate the event. Ice put it on over his jean jacket so he looked like the Incredible Hulk. When the bar tab came Art turned to me and said, "Shel, I'm light, can you cover me?" Yeah, I covered the big spender. As Ice and Jack staggered down the street on the way back home, I heard some student yell, "Hey, that's my professor. He's shit-faced!" I wonder if Ice still has that shirt, because it's a memento of a big night that I'm sure he doesn't remember.

Ice has not remarried, but he has always been able to sweet-talk attractive women. He even had a beautiful Indian girl-friend for a time (he said he was taken in by her *bindi*), but I think she might have tired of his relentless negativity, kind of like Alvy in *Annie Hall*: "I feel that life is divided into the horrible and the miserable. That's the two categories. The horrible are like, I don't know, terminal cases, you know, and blind people, crippled. I don't know how they get through life. It's amazing to me. And the miserable is everyone else. So you should be thankful that you're miserable, because that's very lucky, to be miserable." That's Ice, bless his heart.

I owe Ice for my most improbable "brush with greatness," one that disarms anyone else who tries to top it. In 1992 Ice organized a conference on Muhammad Ali, one of the most famous sportsmen of all time. Ice invited The Champ to come to Oxford; surprisingly he showed up with his photographer and longtime friend, Howard Bingham. At the dinner reception after the conference, I sat next to The Champ, who despite his worsening Parkinson's disease (they used to call it "punch drunk") did a couple of little magic tricks for me. He loved those, but it was tough to see the trembling hands and hear the slurred speech of the once elegant and glib boxer. Then Ali pulled out a Koran and started reading a passage, evidently trying to convince me that Islam belonged in my life. "Muham-mad," I responded wryly, "my father is a Lutheran minister." He laughed and said, "Uh oh, he's not going to like this."

It was a sad day for me when Ice left Miami for a Big Ten university; I have never replaced his friendship. The unhappy but funny Jew from California and the naive Norwegian Lutheran from Minnesota had a special bond. The Miami WAC would never be the same.

Ice started a new WAC chapter at his new school; we used to challenge each other to see who could get more people to our meetings. Ice's WAC even made it into a legal proceeding, but not for any criminal behavior. When Ice's history department denied tenure to a woman assistant professor, she sued the university. In her deposition she accused the men in the department of conspiring against her in something called the "Wednesday Athletic Club." Needless to say she lost the case, because, as any WACer can tell you, the club is ecumenical and tolerant, with an equal opportunity policy for any and all miscreants, regardless of gender, class, race, or sexual preference.

Ice has since moved on. An Ivy League grad, he always aspired to return to the big dance. But, alas, Ice found "nuttin'" at the Ivy League school and returned to the Midwest to teach in Chicago. He's happy in the Windy City, and yes, he's a Cubs fan. Ice and the tragic loser Cubs fit each other like hand and glove, but then they had to go and win a World Series in 2016.

As my colleagues at Miami get older, crankier, and deafer, it's tough to get them out for a couple of drinks. The younger ones have kids, and the new academics are way too serious— often thinking there is some ulterior motive to anything you say or do. I have recast the WAC—into its fifth decade now—as the old German *Stammtisch*, frequented by grad students or seniors in my history seminars. After they hear about the long and storied history of the WAC, they are thrilled to be part of the wacky club.

The new WACer intramural softballers at Minnesota were as good as the Wild Turkeys were bad. Our pitcher was history major Ted Mondale, the son of U.S. vice president Walter Mondale. As a senator from Minnesota, Walter Mondale embodied the ethos of the state. Minnesota is as close to a Scandinavian social democracy as any state in the union. Walter is a mild-mannered Norwegian imbued with a deep commitment to the common good, to the idea that everyone's happiness depends on the economic and social health of all the people, not just a select few.

When his father ran for president in 1984, Ted asked me to house-sit Walter's residence in suburban St. Paul. It was rumored that the strange house had been inspired by Frank Lloyd Wright; none of the walls were at a right angle. It was like living on the set of the great expressionist silent film *The Cabinet of Dr. Caligari*.

Walter lost in a landslide to incumbent President Ronald Reagan in 1984, in part because he suggested that taxes would have to be raised to cover Reagan's budget deficits. In the end Reagan *did* raise some taxes, just as Mondale predicted, but few Republicans remember that. The "no new taxes" pledge has been the gospel of the Republican Party ever since. Walter Mondale is an honest and good man, but as I quipped to our team after Ted had lined a ball that landed just foul of the left field line, "Typical Mondale—just a little bit too far to the left." That was a low blow.

Ted and his sister, Eleanor, were rambunctious kids. If there had been today's ubiquitous social media back then, they might have gotten their dad in a lot of trouble. After the games Ted was always in the middle of WACer mischief.

The WACers won a couple of intramural coed softball championships not because we men were that good, but because our women were always better than the other team's women. When I was teaching high school history in the mid-1970s, I coached the field events for Hopkins High School's track-and-field team. Dee and Deb were 6'3" twins on that team, and they were outstanding all-around athletes. They were among the first women to benefit from Title IX legislation, which mandated equal subsidies for men and women athletes at public schools. Both Dee and Deb played D-1 basketball; I found Dee a basketball job in Germany. I recruited them for the WACers. We also had a tough broad at first base (she would consider that a compliment) who would mock my hardest throws from shortstop as "wimpy, wimpy."

12. The WAC softball team at the Polish Tournament in Browerville, Minnesota. Paul the Wall is standing on the right, Randy is kneeling far right, and Brad Lundell is holding up a goose egg against the scoreboard. I am kneeling second from the left, and the vice president's son Ted Mondale is to my left trying to goose me. Dark Dick is behind Ted. Courtesy of the author.

I also put together a pretty good intramural basketball team, featuring Ted and Lisa, another advisee in the history department. She had played point guard for the Lady Gophers, and by the time I met her she had used up her eligibility. What a find Lisa was for our men's team. When I went to Poland to do research for my dissertation in 1987, I brokered a deal for her to play ball in West Berlin.

Those women were my role models. Years later when my daughter leaned toward doing dance, I steered her toward playing basketball and softball. Except for excellent hand-eye skills, Lauren didn't have above average athletic ability, but she became a very good shooter in high school and an excellent fast-pitch softball catcher. Randy calls her "Yogi," after the great Yankee catcher Lawrence "Yogi" Berra. My

Yogi was the smartest kid on the field—calling the pitches and defensive plays. She always knew how many outs there were and where the ball was supposed to go. Was it wrong for me to want her to get down and dirty with the "tools of ignorance" rather than to flit around in a tutu? Given all of the signals that bombard young women about how they should look, I have no regrets. Yogi doesn't either.

Pat, the center on our intramural team, was a brilliant but somewhat touched Harvard-bred economics professor. At 6'8" and 225 pounds he dominated the paint, but Pat often became unhinged on the court. He's the only guy I've ever played with who got a technical foul for yelling at one of his *own* players. This might be an unfair critique of his scholarship, but he was one of those devotees of the "rational expectations" school of economics. Unfortunately Wall Street traders and investors don't always do the legal and "expected"; the complex causes of 2008 financial collapse, as Margot Robbie explains to us from the bathtub in the movie *The Big Short*, were anything but rational, at least in the legal sense.

I also started playing baseball again in a league for people over thirty-five. Dark Dick (he was a very serious guy), a writer for Randy at *City Pages*, decided to put a team together. Dark Dick was a baseball legend at tiny Clarissa High School in northern Minnesota. On the way to our lake home I pass the Clarissa baseball field on Highway 71 and always joke, "There it is. The house the Dark Dick built."

Bossen Park in south Minneapolis was our home field, so we called ourselves the Southside Johnnies, after Southside Johnny and the Asbury Jukes, one of Bruce Springsteen's Jersey buddy bands. Randy, Dick, and I were the core of the team. Dick was a wily pitcher, I played short, and Randy second. We didn't have enough players, so Dick put an ad in the classifieds and came up with an old Cuban to play first and a Mexican American catcher. In hot weather we had to make sure that the Cuban sat down, lest he have a heat stroke.

13. The Southside Johnnies. Owner, general manager, manager, and pitcher Dark Dick is standing far left. Fellow historian Dr. Tom Jones is kneeling second from the left. My best friend Dave Smith, who played against me at Hamline University, is kneeling third from the left. My Augsburg teammate and longtime dentist Dr. John Ewert is kneeling far right. Our Cuban recruit Eddy Herrera is declaring us number one. Courtesy of the author.

We added other guys we knew, most of them basketball players like my Augsburg teammate John Ewert and Dave Smith, who played for coach Howie Schultz at Hamline. Baseball connoisseurs will remember Wally Pipp, the Yankee first baseman Lou Gehrig replaced to start his fifteen-year iron man record. Schultz was the first baseman Jackie Robinson replaced when he broke the color barrier with the Brooklyn Dodgers in 1947. Who knew? The Johnnies averaged about 6'3", and I always thought it was funny that the other teams we played were so short. The Johnnies didn't hit much, but we played good defense and were the only guys in the league who stole bases and put plays on.

One of the guys on the team knew the anchor on the most-watched Twin City nightly news show. The newscaster shall remain nameless because years later I heard that he did not think this story was funny. He claimed he was a pitcher, so we let him throw a game for the Johnnies. He did okay, but had a lot of help from our defense. It was the first game he had thrown in years, so I kept coming in from short to ask him if he had had enough. "No" was his answer every time. He probably threw 120 pitches in six innings. That night on the ten o'clock newscast, his fellow anchor commented at one point that the papers on her desk were all wet. Our pitcher had an ice pack on his aching shoulder and it was melting all over her copy. His arm was shot and he never threw for the Johnnies again.

I was an All-City shortstop at South High, but I was all field, no hit. I hit a miserable .230 in my senior year. Years later I might have found out why. During an eye exam, out of the blue the ophthalmologist asked me if I had ever played baseball. I said, "Yes, and I hit like shit, even though I have played the game my whole life." He had noticed that as an object came close to my eyes, one wandered off the target. I had no depth perception on a ball coming at me. With the Johnnies I completely changed my batting stance from the upright Mickey Mantle to the crouching, open-stanced Nellie Fox. Voilà! I saw the ball better and even hit it now and then.

I owe my PhD to a wonderful coterie of professors at Minnesota. My adviser was Richard Rudolph, a noted scholar of East European social and economic history. Rudolph looked like Beethoven—short, rotund, with a round face and hair awry. One time Rick pointedly told me that I had misspelled his name: "It's Rudolph, not Rudolf." The former was the Jewish spelling, and he did *not* want to be mistaken for someone of German heritage.

One of my other mentors in the history department was a diplomatic historian who fit the stereotype of the eccentric, absentminded professor. He could act out a brilliant, fifty-minute lecture on twentieth-century European diplomatic history without ever referring to notes; of course in those days there was no such thing as PowerPoint. That professor was a one-man show, mesmerizing students with his stories of the Hohenzollern Kaisers, Hitler's gang, or Stalin's brutality. He embellished the narrative for dramatic effect, which gave his graduate assistants plenty of fodder to chew on in the weekly discussion sections. We had to clarify stuff like "Stalin admired Hitler" or "I wonder why Germans are so much more cultured than Poles." He was an unapologetic Germanophile (except for Hitler, of course, whom he saw as an accident of German history).

Every seat in his classes was filled; as he left the lecture hall on the last day of the semester he always got a standing ovation, befitting a great performance after the final act of a Shakespearean play. I have always craved that applause after my last class, but, alas, I am still waiting. I am not in his thespian league.

That professor's one book on Belgian neutrality appeared in 1972. His large lecture courses were a big recruiting tool for the history department, but his colleagues gave him little respect because he didn't publish another monograph. He should have been given more classes to teach because that was his gift. He loved the great stories of history, even if they were sweetened up. He was an "old school" historian, working on narratives of European diplomatic, political, and biographical "dead white guy" history.

All of those genres have fallen out of favor in the profession; history departments are losing more and more students and faculty as a result. When I left Minnesota, the department was gravitating away from grand old narratives toward sociological history, a numbers game of demographic records and economic determinism. Traditionally history has been in the humanities, but at the University of Minnesota it was part of the social sciences division, and housed on the sixth floor of the Social Science Tower on the West Bank of the university.

I was a teaching assistant for one American history professor who did not mention ten names in his survey course on

U.S. history. He was an excellent scholar and a good friend, but his lectures were as uninspired as the diplomatic historian's were electric. I don't remember much about that course or about U.S. economic and demographic trends from one decade to the next.

Rumor had it that one time the great teacher and orator had a mental breakdown during a lecture on the Night of the Long Knives, when Hitler purged the Nazi Party of all opposition. He began ranting and raving while brandishing a plastic machine gun as though he were gunning down SA chief Ernst Röhm. In these days of mass murders on campus, students would duck and run for cover, but the graduate students calmly took him by the elbow and escorted him out of the hall.

I was unconvinced of the veracity of this tale until I called him one day about some grading I was doing for his course. He asked where I was calling from, and when I told him Walter Mondale's house, he was sure that the line was bugged: "Did you hear that? Did you hear that click? This line is being tapped." I rolled my eyes and thought about conducting the rest of the conversation in German, which we both spoke fluently.

There were other characters in the Social Science Tower who were equally neurotic. I played on the history department's softball team (we were terrible) with one noted scholar of Brazilian history. The diminutive professor should have taught French revolutionary history because he had a huge Napoleon complex. He hated to lose at anything. When we played tennis, over and over he would call my shot "out" when the ball was several inches in.

Political scientists are another breed altogether. It was a dysfunctional department at Miami for years. The political science department at Minnesota occupied the top floor of the eight-story Social Science Tower. The political scientists probably liked the symbolism of their perch atop the other departments (including history), but catching one of the building's three elevators was a daily aggravation.

One day the down elevator opened and a notoriously surly political science professor swore at me under his breath for taking too much time getting on. Although I was a lowly graduate student, I turned to him and said angrily, "What is your problem? What *is* your problem?" He grunted and muttered something under his breath. I generalize, but political scientists are as a whole an ornery bunch because they think that there is some self-serving power play behind every human action. Given the state of American politics today, I guess I understand their cynicism. But they don't have to carry that over into everyday life.

Nearly twenty years later, I was getting on a flight home after an academic conference in Washington DC. I was one of the last passengers on the plane, and I had to ask the aisle and middle seat occupants to let me into my window seat. When the old guy in the aisle seat mumbled something about having to stand up to let me by, I gave him a disdainful stare as if to say, "What is your problem?" Incredibly, it was the same political science professor from Minnesota. I told the woman in the middle seat about our previous encounter and this improbable coincidence.

Fortunately I did not have to take a course from that misanthrope, but political science courses were cognates for my degree in European history. The political science courses I took were highly theoretical, and the seminar discussions were loaded with political science jargon. I was the only historian in those courses. One particularly verbose and confident political science PhD candidate dazzled me with his erudite exegesis of foreign policy theory. I had no idea what the hell he was talking about. Toward the end of the semester, after one of his particularly lengthy discourses, one of the other students asked him, "What are you trying to say?" The pedant stammered and stuttered, then blurted out, "I don't know." I felt a lot better and a lot smarter after that, and knew that I had made the right choice to study history.

Content analysis, game theory, and independent and dependent variables were not for me.

In those days two languages were required for a PhD in history at Minnesota. I was fluent in German, so I needed to take Polish. Every day I walked three-quarters of a mile across the Washington Avenue Bridge over the Mississippi to Polish class with Dr. Leonard Polakiewicz, a well-known scholar of Anton Chekhov, the great nineteenth-century Russian writer.

Polakiewicz was a jovial, proud Polish American who was delighted that the few students in his class wanted to learn Polish, as though it were some endangered indigenous language. The wind gets very cold on that bridge high above the river, which seemed just right for those of us studying Soviet and East European history. The more I studied Polish and the tragic history of Eastern Europe in the twentieth century—a region that one historian of World War II called "the bloodlands"—the less I complained about those frigid daily treks. Studying the past, especially the history of an area that experienced two horrible world wars and Soviet oppression during the Cold War, casts perspective on one's own life. Was I suffering on those cold walks over the Mississippi? No.

With the help of those outstanding professors, in 1985 I began working on my dissertation on Poland's economic relations with the United States in the early Cold War. Most historians of U.S. diplomatic history at the time focused on American actors without doing research from the other side. I was determined to get a more complete picture by researching in Polish archives. Getting into the communist country to do that was going to be a problem. Improbably, basketball drew open the Iron Curtain for me.

7

Basketball behind the Iron Curtain

I n 1987 I began to explore the possibility of doing research in the Polish People's Republic. Few western scholars had been allowed access to Polish communist party documents, and my PhD dissertation would be groundbreaking if I could get into Polish archives. I had reason to think that the Polish authorities would agree with the premise of my work, which was that after World War II the communist government wanted to trade with Western Europe, which desperately needed Polish coal for economic recovery.

Contrary to the notion that Stalin was an uncompromising, totalitarian dictator, he did not envision the complete isolation of his sphere of influence from the West, especially economically. Stalin's main objective after World War II was not to spread communism but to secure his western border by controlling Central Europe. Germany had invaded Russia through Poland twice in the first half of the twentieth century; Russia lost almost two million people in World War I and twenty-five million more in World War II. Stalin was not going to let Germany start another war.

Stalin improvised policy in other countries that eventually fell behind the Iron Curtain, but there was no question that he would impose Kremlin-friendly communist governments in the Soviet zone of Germany and Poland. The Polish election of January 1947 was clearly rigged in favor of the communists. Nonetheless the Stalinist government continued to trade with the West. Polish coal made a significant contribution to the success of the Marshall Plan, the U.S. aid program for Western Europe from 1948 to 1952.

I applied to several agencies for a dissertation research grant and got a couple of interviews, even one with the prestigious Fulbright Program, but they all turned me down. I mistakenly assumed that the rejections were due to the rudimentary state of my Polish, not because of the quality of my dissertation proposal or the grant agencies' doubts that the Polish authorities would let me into the archives to see sensitive documents.

Instead I took an offer to play basketball in Lublin and then wormed my way into the archives with help from my good friend Wojciech Roszkowski, a prolific scholar of several tomes on Polish history. My dissertation adviser at Minnesota put me in touch with Roszkowski, who headed the prestigious Miller Center at the University of Virginia in the early 2000s. He even had time for politics, winning a seat in the European Parliament in 2004. Roszkowski recently published a three-volume history of the world at the time of Jesus Christ (*Świat Chrystusa*). I am in debt to Roszkowski for convincing the stiff communist apparatchiks to give me access to party documents.

During my stay in Poland I got to know some of the diplomats at the U.S. Embassy in Warsaw. At one embassy cocktail party, the cultural attaché took me aside and said, "I remember you, Sheldon. I was on the Fulbright Committee that rejected your application. We didn't think that the Polish government would let you into the archives, so we turned you down." Although a Fulbright would have looked good on my résumé, I'm glad I didn't get a research grant. The basketball junket was not only fun, but it gave me the opportunity to meet Poles of varied backgrounds (not just academics), to experience everyday life in communist Poland, and to travel all over the country on road trips.

My Polish basketball connection stemmed from a chance meeting with players from Gwardia Wrocław during a tournament in West Germany in 1980. Marian Czajkowski was a phys ed teacher and Zdzisław Rychlewicz a policeman, but neither sympathized with the communist regime. At a banquet for all the tournament teams, none of the Germans were engaging the Gwardia players, so I did. I had taken some beginners' Russian and knew that people in the Soviet satellites were forced to learn Russian as a second language, and that Polish was a related Slavic language.

The Poles snickered when I greeted them in Russian, not because my Russian was so bad but because an American had opted to try Russian rather than English. Marian and Zdzisław spoke pretty good English, and in the course of the conversation they invited me to visit Poland. They even suggested that I play a season in Wrocław, but I was unable to make the connections necessary to make the move. Telephoning from West Germany to Poland was difficult in those days, and letters took weeks. It was a missed opportunity given my eventual focus on Polish history; a year immersed in Polish language and culture would have been invaluable.

In the spring of 1981 I took a train from Munich to Wrocław (Breslau in German), which had been part of Germany before World War II and awarded to Poland in 1945. The Poles expelled most of the Germans from the areas acquired from Germany. Many of the new Wrocław residents were transplanted Poles from prewar Polish territories in the east that had been annexed by the Soviet Union. Poles did not want to end up in the Soviet Union after the war; they were disappointed when Poland was forced into the Soviet bloc.

Of all the countries that fought with the Allies against Hitler in World War II, the Poles were handed the cruelest reward—over forty more years of communist dictatorship. When I visited Marian for a second time in 1987, he took me to the Racławice Panorama, a huge 140-meter cycloramic painting that had also migrated from the former eastern Polish city of Lwów (present-day Lviv in Ukraine) after World War II. The painting had been commissioned in 1894 to commemorate General Tadeusz Kościuszko's victory over the Russians at Racławice a hundred years earlier. Kościuszko also contributed to the victory of George Washington's Revolutionary Army, but the 1794 Polish insurrection against Russian rule eventually failed. The Polish communist authorities considered the painting too nationalistic and anti-Russian, and did not allow its showing until 1985.

Poland was in the throes of political upheaval during my first trip in 1981. After negotiating a deal with the communist government in August 1980, the free trade union Solidarity grew to encompass nearly a third of the population, including many communist party members. The economy was in shambles and rogue elements in Solidarity were calling for wildcat strikes and demanding real political freedom. The Kremlin told the Polish communist party to bring the situation under control; in December 1981 the government declared martial law and Solidarity was outlawed.

Unlike the claustrophobic feeling I had during visits to communist East Germany, Poland seemed like a free country. From the summer of 1980 to the banning of Solidarity, Poles were bursting with enthusiasm about their newfound freedom to discuss Polish history. The Marxists had warped it to such an extent that the Soviet Union was cast as the Polish people's best friend. A central theme of these frank discussions was Stalin's betrayal of Poland before, during, and after World War II, and the illegitimacy of the current, Kremlin-backed Polish regime.

The Polish communists simply omitted discussion of the Soviet Union's relations with Poland during World War II. In 1980 Poles were now filling in the blanks about Stalin's partition of Poland with Hitler a week before the German attack on September 1, 1939; the Soviets' murder of thousands of Polish army officers in the Katyn Forest in 1940; Stalin's denial of aid to the Polish uprising against the Germans in Warsaw in 1944; and his imposition of the communist regime in Poland. The Red Army's "liberation" of Poland was a bitter pill. At the time I had only marginal knowledge of these events. Marian excitedly related each story to me.

Marian and Zdzisław were thrilled to have an American visitor. Poland has had close historical connections to the United States. In the nineteenth century, when the Polish nation had no state, Poles looked to France and the republican ideas of the Enlightenment for inspiration to resurrect Poland. In the twentieth century Poland looked to the United States for liberation, in part because of the millions of Poles who had emigrated to America. It is said that Chicago is the second largest Polish city, after Warsaw.

When President Woodrow Wilson issued U.S. war aims during World War I, Poles were the *only* people singled out to get a new independent state (the thirteenth of Wilson's Fourteen Points). There are streets in Poland named after Wilson, but none for President Franklin Roosevelt. Poles wrongly blame Roosevelt for appeasing Stalin at the Yalta Conference, held at a time when the war in both Europe and Asia was still raging. At that point the western Allies could not afford to press Stalin on political issues. The Red Army would determine Poland's fate anyway. Short of starting a new war against his Soviet ally, there was nothing Roosevelt could have done to ensure that Poland got a freely elected, democratic government after the war. Poland's fate was determined by its geostrategic position.

Marian and Zdzisław took me to one of Gwardia's basketball practices, where we played against three other players on the club. Marian had utter contempt for the communists; he took me aside before the game and said that one guy on the other team was a government agent. Suddenly this was not just a basketball game but a political contest. I was the American representing democracy, capitalism, and the freedom that Poland had been promised at the end of the war but didn't get. I thought it was cool that my job was to beat a Marxist. Much to Marian's delight, we won every game. It was these little victories over the oppressors that kept people in the Soviet bloc going.

After practice, the players, communist or not, were more concerned about scoring some suds, but the local bar did not have any beer. I didn't know any Polish at the time, but I quickly became familiar with the term *nie ma*, meaning "there isn't any." Chronic shortages of consumer goods were the norm in the communist countries. Whenever a Polish restaurant or pub did not have something on the menu, the waiter would utter a quick "nie ma." Poles were used to it, but this time the Gwardia players accused the barkeep of hoarding beer for party members or privileged customers who were willing to pay a surcharge. The players tried to call the local party authorities, but to no avail. We went home thirsty. I found the Poles to be most gracious hosts; the players wanted to show the American a good time. This incident was embarrassing for them.

The whole Polish economy was in trouble during that summer of Solidarity in 1981. It seemed the only commodity in abundant supply was strawberries. Solidarity had wrested some concessions out of the government, but the political uncertainty pushed an already strained economy to the breaking point. Poles had lived relatively well in the 1970s off of loans from the West. The Warsaw train station was one of the finest in the Soviet bloc, but it was built on credit. Some $21 billion in loans was coming due. Divisions within Solidarity, the government's indecisiveness, and wildcat strikes sent the economy into a tailspin.

Nonetheless Marian and Zdzisław decided to take me on an arduous, one-day pilgrimage to Kraków, which is about two hundred kilometers east of Wrocław. Kraków is Poland's most beautiful old city. Unlike Warsaw, it was largely undamaged in the war. In 1993 I took a group of Miami University students on a tour of Prague, Kraków, Auschwitz, and Warsaw. They loved the romantic beauty of Prague and Kraków, were humbled by Auschwitz, but disappointed in Warsaw. They asked me why we had come there. "History," I replied.

To understand the suffering of Poland in World War II, the students not only had to see Auschwitz but Warsaw, the beautiful old capital that the Germans had destroyed in the war. The Germans bombed Warsaw in 1939, obliterated the Warsaw Jewish Ghetto in 1943, and razed most of the city during the Warsaw Uprising in 1944. The Red Army was right across the Vistula River in 1944 when the Polish Home Army rose up against the Germans, but Stalin did not move to support this Polish rebellion, which was backed by the West-friendly Polish exiled government in London. Stalin let the Germans destroy the armed wing of the London Poles, who opposed his puppet Polish communist government. Given what Stalin had done to Poland, it was impossible for a Polish patriot to support that regime.

More damage was done to Warsaw when the Red Army took it in early 1945. The Polish communist government rebuilt a few blocks of the old town, but the state did not have the resources to restore the splendor of prewar Warsaw. The gray ugliness of socialist reinforced-concrete architecture pounded home the lesson to my history students.

Marian and I wedged into Zdzisław's "miały [little] Fiat" for the eight-hour, one-day round trip to Kraków to see Wawel Hill. Staying in a hotel was too expensive for them. In the fifties the Italian car company had contracted with Poland to manufacture Fiat models in Poland. This tiny car was smaller than a Volkswagen Beetle. When I was playing ball in Poland six years later, Wojciech Roszkowski and I picked up my basketball buddy Roger Anderson from the Warsaw airport in Wojciech's Fiat. I have no idea how the 6'10" center from Notre Dame got into that mini-car.

The Fiat was a workhorse, but Zdzisław's old model was hard pressed to make the long trip to Kraków with three guys over 6'2". The car repeatedly overheated and gas was hard to come by in that summer of Solidarity. We filled up extra gas cans whenever we found an open service station.

14. Notre Dame alum and longtime basketball buddy Roger Anderson on his visit to see the author in Warsaw in 1988. Wojciech Roszkowski and I picked up the 6'10" center at the airport in Wojciech's little Fiat. Courtesy of the author.

Wawel Hill is one of the most hallowed historical sites in Poland. Many of the important kings and queens of Poland are buried in the cathedral there, including Jan Sobieski, the savior of Vienna against the invading Turks in 1683, and General Józef Piłsudski, who helped resurrect Poland after World War I. He became Poland's most revered twentieth-century leader, although many historians are critical of him for establishing a dictatorship in 1926. The names on most of the tombs were unfamiliar to me except for one: Kościuszko, the symbol of the Poles' heroic struggles against foreign oppression.

That trip to Kraków in 1981 inspired me to study Polish history. It was a labor of love for those two ballplayers to take me there. They were not historians. I can't think of any historical site in the United States where Americans would feel compelled to take a foreign visitor on such a difficult trip.

It was readily apparent that Poles have a deep reverence for their history, much of which is bathed in blood and suffering. Americans tend to approach history in a vastly different way. Many are indifferent to the past; the new is revered and the old is forgotten or ignored. Some Germans would rather forget their recent history, but the country has honestly dealt with the dark Nazi era.

Poles are generally consumed with their past and defending their national honor. They often view frank historical discussions as political debates. In 2009 I gave a talk to a Polish American audience on Polish communist leader General Wojciech Jaruzelski's imposition of martial law and the banning of Solidarity in December 1981. News had just come out about Jaruzelski's request for Soviet help in suppressing the movement; there was talk about whether that was a treasonous act. I was met with hostility when I said that this supposed "smoking gun" of Jaruzelski's betrayal of Poland was not surprising because, from its creation in 1944, the Polish communist government had always relied on Soviet backing. The Polish American audience wanted me to condemn him.

Other historians have often asked me if I have any Polish roots, as if that would be the reason for my interest in Polish history. "No," I reply, "I'm 100 percent Norwegian." I go on to say that in some ways that makes me a more objective chronicler of Poland's past. The passionate defense of personal agendas is a big problem in the historical profession. All historians have biases, but the best strive to overcome them with sober, honest analysis of the past. I have no ax to grind when it comes to defending Poland's heritage. I often kid that the Swedes are the big enemy for my Norwegians, because until 1905 Norway was governed by the Swedish king. I call it "oppression lite."

The more I studied East European history the more I realized that many histories of the region were political treatises as much as evidentiary chronicles. Years ago at a history conference session on Poland in World War II, one of the most highly respected American historians of modern Polish history, a woman of Polish descent, declared that it was a myth that the Polish Army met the German blitzkrieg in

1939 with cavalry charges. Those stories cast the Poles as heroic in defense of their country, but also as a backward people with nineteenth-century military strategy and out-moded tools of war. She said that Poles on horseback did not take on Wehrmacht panzers.

An elderly Polish American woman in the audience stood up and said, "I was a young girl when the Germans attacked Poland. I saw the Polish Army on horses fighting tanks." The historian was taken aback and did not have a response. Now it could be that the woman had seen the Poles using horses as transport and not in battle, but who knows? I tell my students to never say never when it comes to history. As careful as I am to paint an accurate picture of the past, I have made mistakes; I'm glad that I'm a PhD and not an MD whose slip-ups can jeopardize a person's health.

The moral of the story is that histories written with a political agenda are always suspect. Nationalists defend their people as though they have never committed a collective wrong. During the Yugoslav civil war in the mid-1990s, a Bosnian Serb woman in my class vehemently objected to my statement that although atrocities had been committed by all sides—Bosnian Croats, Bosniaks (Slavic Muslims), and Bosnian Serbs—the last bore the brunt of the blame, because they had greater manpower, firepower, and the backing of the former Yugoslav Army (largely Serb). After all it was Bosnian Serb forces who besieged Sarajevo and lobbed mortars to terrorize the city. The Bosnian Serb massacre of more than eight thousand Bosniaks at Srebrenica is undeniable.

The student came storming into my office to defend the Bosnian Serbs, saying that western press reports were slanted against them. The inherent bias she alleged of western journalists didn't make sense, because the Serbs were Orthodox Christians and Serbia had fought on the side of the United States in both world wars. In 1995 the United States and NATO came to the defense of the Bosniaks to stop the bloodshed.

If I was going to criticize her people, the student was going to criticize mine. That's what nationalists do—think in terms of the collective good of their country and the bad of the other. She pointed out that the United States had a history of slavery and had killed millions in the war in Vietnam. I disarmed her by admitting that what she said was true.

Martyrdom is an important part of the Serb national consciousness. Their national holiday is a fourteenth-century *defeat* by the Turks. Likewise Poles suffer from an inferiority complex because of their long history of oppression, and tend to defend their national honor vehemently when it is questioned. Poles have called their country "The Christ of Nations"—a country that has suffered on the cross throughout their modern history. Poland was one of the most important countries of Europe in the seventeenth century, but a weak monarchy, lack of internal cohesion, and foreign intrigue ended in partition of the state at the end of the eighteenth century.

Kościuszko's failed uprising against Russia resulted in the demise of the Polish state in 1795. For 123 years the Poles were variously subjects of the Prussian-German, Austrian, and Russian empires. Polish historians highlight the brave uprisings against the Russian czar in 1830 and 1863, and emphasize the Piłsudski-led Polish army's "armed deed" to forge the new independent state in 1918. Poles often lay blame on the French and British for the collapse of the Polish army to the German attack in 1939 because Poland's western allies had appeased Hitler over and over; even though they finally declared war on Poland's behalf, they gave Warsaw little military help.

The pockmarks on the surviving old buildings in central Warsaw bear silent witness to the German destruction of the city in World War II. Numerous memorials remind Varsovians of the Warsaw Uprising in 1944. On All Saints' Day Poles light thousands of candles in cemeteries to commemorate lost loved ones; during communist rule impromptu memorials popped up to remember the Soviet massacre of Polish soldiers at the Katyn Forest in 1940, when Stalin was still in partnership with Hitler.

In 1984 Polish secret security agents murdered Father Jerzy Popiełuszko because he was an outspoken supporter of Solidarity. In the courtyard of his church in northern Warsaw stood small stone monuments to the victims of the Nazi concentration and death camps. On a visit to the church I noticed that a monument to Katyn was set among them. It is unclear whether the monument was placed there to put Katyn victims in the same category as the dead at Auschwitz or Treblinka, or as a thinly veiled protest against the Soviets and the Polish communist government. Maybe both. Uprisings against the Polish communist regime in 1956 and 1976 resulted in scores of dead, spawning new days of remembrance.

Three million Jews lived in Poland at the beginning of the war, the largest population of Jews in Europe. The Nazi-run death camps were all located in Poland, calling into question how much the Poles, who were subject to Nazi tyranny as well, were willing to go to the aid of the Jews. It is patently unfair to criticize the Poles, who themselves were trying to survive the brutal German occupation, but some Polish historians were adamant in their denunciation of Jan Gross's 2001 book about Polish atrocities against Jews in the town of Jedwabne in 1940. The debate goes on about which country in interwar Europe was the most anti-Semitic. The Catholic Poles were not known for their tolerance, but as World War II broke out what country could claim to treat its minorities justly? That included the United States, still entrenched in Jim Crowism.

My histories of Poland are not framed in terms of defending its good name. Poland was in charge of its own fate in the prewar period. The Poles had more freedom of movement on the diplomatic front than is commonly assumed. The Poles relied on France and Britain for their survival, but the western Allies were of no help diplomatically or militarily. Warsaw could choose between closer relations with Berlin or Moscow, admittedly both bad choices. However, Polish foreign minister Józef Beck chose to curry the favor of the Third Reich. The best option would have been for Warsaw to build a bloc of Central European states to thwart Hitler—Czechoslovakia, Hungary, Romania, and Yugoslavia. But when Chamberlain and Daladier handed over the Sudetenland to Hitler at Munich in 1938, instead of siding with the beleaguered Czechoslovaks the Poles gobbled up the city of Cieszyn (Teschen) on the Polish-Czechoslovak border. Together, Czechoslovakia and Poland could have mustered a strong defense against Nazi aggression in 1938.

The Polish Home Army's uprising against the Germans in 1944 was certainly heroic, but it was a futile loss of tens of thousands of Polish lives. Fighting the Germans was hopeless unless the Red Army came to the rescue, which was wishful thinking. Stalin had no intention of allowing the Home Army and the Polish exiled government in London to forge an independent Poland after the war.

The thesis of my dissertation, which was that the Polish communist government cooperated with Western Europe economically in the late 1940s, often fell on the deaf ears of Polish nationalists.

Stymied in my attempts to get a grant to do research in Warsaw, in 1987 I contacted Marian and Zdzisław about the possibility of playing basketball in Poland. They gave me the name of the manager of AZS (Academic Sports Union) Lublin, a second-league team affiliated with the state-run Lublin University. Lublin is a backwater city in the southeast of Poland, but four centuries earlier it was an important crossroads in the Polish state. The Union of Lublin in 1569 forged the Kingdom of Poland and the Grand Duchy of Lithuania into a single polity.

As the Red Army was moving into Poland in 1944, Stalin formed the Lublin Committee as the core of Poland's postwar communist government. The Soviet leader once said that imposing communism in Poland was like saddling a cow. He was probably referring in part to the power of the Polish Catholic Church; the communist government had to treat the church with kid gloves so as not to rouse the ire of devout Polish Catholics. The Catholic University of Lublin was the only independent university in the Soviet bloc.

Karol Wojtyła was a member of the university's department of Christian philosophy in the 1950s. He was elected Pope John Paul II in 1978, the first non-Italian pope in over four centuries. The Polish pope was a serious spiritual challenge to the communist regimes in Eastern Europe. Although there is no definitive evidence, it is likely that Soviet intelligence agencies knew about the assassination attempt on the pope in 1981, if they were not directly behind it.

The pope visited the university in June 1987, shortly before I got to Lublin. AZS Lublin's manager, Darek Baran, showed me his video of the visit, which was a sensation for the city. It was also a sign of the weakness of the Polish regime, which by that time was under pressure from Soviet premier Mikhail Gorbachev to make significant political and economic reforms.

Baran was excited about the prospect of bringing an American player to the club. He offered to get a visa for me to stay in Poland for the season, a dorm room, and vouchers to buy dinner at a local restaurant. He could not procure meat ration cards for me. Without any other options to breach the Iron Curtain, I took the offer to, in effect, shoot and dribble my way to a PhD. I don't think any of the professors on my doctoral committee at Minnesota knew how I got into Poland.

Before I went to Poland that fall, I stopped off in West Germany. I knew it would be difficult to buy things in Poland, so I packed carefully. As I was getting on the train from Hannover to Warsaw, a German friend gave me a Swiss army knife. I doubt that the neutral Swiss have ever carried that ingenious little tool into battle, but it turned out to be one of my most prized possessions. I was on the road a lot with the team that season, and frequently commuted back and forth from Lublin to Warsaw to do research. That clever device opened cans, bottles, and wine; cut cheese and bread; and spread butter and jam.

The other indispensable items I packed were my basketball shoes, contact lenses, one of the first portable computers—a Zenith laptop—and a small Sony radio. Lublin is nearly five hundred miles east of Berlin, but I could catch a faint radio signal from the American armed forces radio service in West Berlin. I always thought that the only good thing about the Cold War was that the Americans still had troops in Germany. Improbably, in the fall of 1987, my Minnesota Twins made it to the World Series. I got up in the middle of the night to listen into all seven games. After all no Minnesota professional team had won a championship since the Lakers took the NBA title thirty-three years before. Minnesota pro teams had come in second six times since then; two presidential candidates from Minnesota (Vice Presidents Hubert Humphrey and Walter Mondale) lost their elections, too. I was jumping around alone at 4 a.m. in my little dorm room in Lublin when the Twins won the World Series.

The Zenith computer had two floppy disk drives, one for the WordPerfect program and the other for saving files. It was about five times as heavy as a much more powerful laptop today, but it was a workhorse. The first time I plugged the computer and voltage converter into a Polish electrical outlet I held my breath. To my great relief, it worked.

That computer was a real curiosity. Few Poles had seen anything like it. Before becoming Soviet premier, Gorbachev had visited the West. He knew that the communist countries were far behind the West in technology of this kind. In the late 1980s he initiated *glasnost* and *perestroika* (openness and economic restructuring) to catch up, opening up honest information about the problems of the command economies and allowing some private market mechanisms. The socialist economies could not retool fast enough; when Gorbachev decided not to use tanks to prop up the Soviet satellite regimes, they collapsed.

My basketball shoes were also a coveted item. My Lublin teammates played in cheap canvas basketball shoes made in Red China, a poor facsimile of the obsolete Converse All-Stars. The players had to skate around in those Sino-shoes because a sharp cut would blow them out. I knew that we would have a big advantage over the other teams in the league if I could get some decent shoes. Fitz was selling Avia basketball shoes at the time; I had my girlfriend (now wife), Kristie, ship over ten pairs. The guys on the team couldn't believe their good fortune in getting those shoes, and did not know how to thank me.

I also had Kristie send over T-shirts for the team emblazoned with the AZS Lublin symbol, a silhouette of the Polish eagle. The communists had removed the crown from the head of the eagle on the official state coat of arms. To them the crown was a symbol of the eighteenth-century Polish monarchy and its interwar, bourgeois-capitalist successor. I had a designer put the crown back on the eagle as a subtle jab at the communist regime. Other than the players on my team, few noticed. Unlike the East Germans, the Polish authorities were indifferent to these minor breaches of socialist etiquette.

The Polish communists ignored the changing of money on the black market as well. Poles repeatedly asked me to exchange Polish zlotys for West German marks or dollars, which for both of us was a good deal. The government banks boosted the zloty's value, so exchanging money there was foolish. I even had government employees asking me to sell hard currency, which Poles could use to travel abroad or shop at the hard currency Pewex stores. Party members and those with connections shopped there for luxury western goods, and average Poles knew it. It was an affront to a system that was ostensibly class-free. I avoided shopping at the Pewex except to buy gifts of wine, coffee, or confections for my friends. I had brought along $700 in cash for the whole season. I lived much better than most Poles, who earned an average of $30 a month.

Baran picked me up at the train station in Warsaw. The team used to kid him that *baran* means sheep or, in Polish slang, an idiot. He was a rotund, energetic, good-hearted, happy guy. He was a mover and shaker who worked the system to bring an American to his team. His wheeling and dealing was typical of many Poles who took advantage of the communist government's laissez-faire attitude toward the black market and low-level corruption.

Strict East German and Czech communists derided Poland for this lackadaisical enforcement of communist rules, and for not being able to run an efficient command economy. The "Polish economy" was a slur that Germans had long used to mock the poverty and alleged laziness of the Poles. Years later I was at a conference of historians in Prague when a Czech scholar got up and complained about Poles repeatedly coming back and forth across the border with Czechoslovakia to make trades. He finished with, "And the Poles are lazy." They sounded like hardworking, ingenious, entrepreneurial types to me.

Baran greeted me warmly and declared that I was going to take AZS Lublin from the second to first Polish basketball league. I laughed to myself because at thirty-six my basketball skills had diminished, and my main reason for coming to Poland was to finish my dissertation research. I did not let on.

Before we drove the two hours to Lublin, we stopped off at the Palace of Culture and Science in Warsaw, where Baran had some business with the national AZS office. The palace was a gift from Stalin, built in what was called wedding-cake style—a mishmash of gaudy Gothic and baroque. It was built in 1952, when the rest of the city still lay in ruins. Most Poles hated this supposed symbol of Soviet friendship—financed by the guy who had partnered with Hitler to partition Poland in 1939. The skyscraper stuck out like a sore thumb or, for Poles, like the middle finger. Every time I took the train to Warsaw I passed by that monstrosity.

There was a buzz at AZS Lublin because of the new American player, a first for the academic club. The local Lublin newspaper wrote that I could be the "great uncle" to the young team and "new energy for AZS." I was one of the few Americans to play basketball in communist Poland. One was Kent Washington from Southampton College, who had played for Start Lublin ten years earlier, another club in the same league as AZS Lublin. Evidently Washington was a great passer and dazzling ball handler, and a big fan favorite. Those skills were not my forte, but I could shoot.

After the long train ride from Hannover to Warsaw and the two-hour drive to Lublin, the team held a practice. I was exhausted from the trip, but the club administration, which was there to see the new American player, was satisfied with my game. They were surprised that I was not Black, like Washington. I suppose that was not surprising because most of the American players in Europe were African Americans, and the NBA was becoming increasingly Black. When my daughter, Lauren, was born I took her two-year-old brother, Max, to see her and their mom in the hospital. As a Black guy passed us in the hall, observant little Max blurted out, "There goes a basketball player."

After our first game in Lublin, a sports reporter from the local newspaper, *Kurier Lubelski*, told me that the AZS fans thought that if an American played basketball, he must be Black. I laughed and joked, "I'm sorry if I disappointed everyone." The reporter was also puzzled that I was playing for a poor university club like AZS and asked if I had tried to play professionally. I told him that I had played in West Germany, but he was dumbfounded that an American would play basketball in communist Poland for no money. That smacked of communism.

Three of the most important national newspapers, *Życie Warszawy* (Warsaw Life), *Przegląd Tygodniowy* (Weekly Review), and *Rzeczpospolita* (The Republic), also picked up my story. On that first day in Warsaw I had not told Baran

● Przez ocean żeby zagrać w kosza

● Przed treningiem korepetycje z polskiego

Amerykanin w Lublinie
czyli
szukanie cykliniarki

NAZWISKO: **Robert Sheldon Anderson**. Narodowość — amerykańska, ale przyznaje się do dziadków z Norwegii. Wzrost — 188 cm. Wiek 36 lat. Kondycja jak u 18-letniego chłopaka. Obowiązkowa mina — uśmiech. Papierosy — broń Boże! Czasami butelka piwa. Profesja — nauczyciel historii. Jeśli znajdzie w lubelskich bibliotekach to czego szuka, będziemy wkrótce zwracali się do niego per „panie doktorze".

● **Kibice myśleli, że jeżeli Amerykanin i gra w koszykówkę to na pewno jest ciemnoskóry...**

— Przykro mi, że rozczarowałem wszystkich, którzy przyszli na pierwszy mecz AZS.

● **Nie żartuj sobie. Dałeś lekcję gry. Gdzie uczyłeś się kozłować piłkę?**

— W moim rodzinnym Minneapolis. To takie miasto nad Missisipi w stanie Minnesota. Mamy tam niezłe uniwersyteckie zespoły.

● **Nie próbowałeś gry za pieniądze?**

— Próbowałem. W zawodowej drużynie Carolina Cougars. Ale chyba byłem za słaby, skoro zrezygnowali ze mnie po tygodniu.

(DOKOŃCZENIE NA STR. 2)

Fot. J. Trembecki

15. Interview in 1988 with the local Polish newspaper *Kurier Lubelski*, wearing a WAC shirt, of course. The headline reads, "American in Lublin Looking for a Floor Sander"—a reference to the slippery wax on the court for my first game with AZS Lublin. Courtesy of the author.

that my main goal was to do research for my dissertation, but I admitted as much in an interview with *Życie Warszawy*. I could easily do both because the team practiced at night and I had all day to work.

A *Przegląd Tygodniowy* reporter was curious about what perks I was getting from the club. He suspected some kind of corruption and illegal under-the-table payments. He asked me where I ate and whether I had meat coupons, a precious commodity in those days. I told him that I shopped at the local state-run grocery store, ate breakfast in my room, lunch at the university dining hall, and dinner at a local restaurant whose selection was very slim. Turkey, potatoes, and gravy were the usual fare. The journalist suspected that I really went to the Pewex to get what I needed. "I don't do that because I want to try to live like you," I replied, "so I can better understand you. But it is really strange that one can buy anything with dollars there [at the Pewex] . . . and that everything can be arranged 'na lewo' [on the black market]."

There is a Polish word that I quickly learned when I needed my Polish friends to take care of something for me—*załatwiac*—to manage or settle (something). Under communism there was little incentive for the state-run enterprises to provide good service, so using connections was the way to get something done. When I caught an elbow to the mouth in one game and needed my lip stitched up, Baran sent me to see a doctor he knew. The doctor was skilled but the sutures looked like twine. I still have that scar.

Someone on the club got me into the best hair salon in Lublin, although the shop only did women's hair. I got snickers from the ladies whenever I came in, but the stylist spent an hour on my coiffure. It was the best haircut I have ever had. I tipped him the same amount as his fee—about two bucks. It was a very good deal for both of us.

For the first few months in Poland I sat in the Lublin University library reading old Polish newspapers on my dissertation topic. It was a good way to hone my language skills in preparation for doing research in the archives in Warsaw. By the time I was ready to go to Warsaw for three days a week, Baran and the club were so happy with me and the team's record that they didn't care if I took a couple of days off from practice. He arranged for me to work out with a team in Warsaw.

I needed a place to stay in Warsaw, so Wojciech Rosz-kowski, my connection to get into the archives, asked his brother, Macek, if he would put me up for two or three days a week. Macek had an apartment in Mokotów, which was fifteen minutes on the tram from the train station and a short walk to the archives.

The family's five-room apartment was already a merry menagerie before I showed up. Basia and Macek had three boys and a daughter, aged five to fifteen, and a cat. Macek ran a sail-making business in the apartment, so several employees came in every day to sew sails, mostly for sale to West German yachtsmen. And there was a Russian living in a tiny room off the kitchen. I guess he made sails, too. Basia spent the whole day in the kitchen, fixing breakfasts and lunches for the family and the crew. She had hot water boiling all day to make tea. The cat had a nasal condition, so she would sit next to the teapot and breathe in the steam. I loved teatime with the stuffed-up cat and Basia, who sadly passed away several years ago.

Macek and Basia generously welcomed me into their extended family, in part because they liked the novelty of having an American in the house. We had no agreement for me to pay rent, but over Macek's vehement objections I gave him some money to stay there. Every week I brought good coffee and chocolate from the Pewex, or a Bulgarian or Hungarian red wine from a state shop. Macek spoke pretty good English, but I spoke Polish with Basia and the rest of the family. It was a great educational opportunity for the kids and for me.

Macek was a sailor, replete with the captain's mutton chops. He built a big sailboat that he kept in Gdańsk. The whole family could sleep in it. Macek always talked about taking me on a voyage to Oslo and the fjords of Norway; I regret not having had the time for a private cruise to my ancestral home.

Wojciech arranged for me to meet with the gruff apparatchik who ran the Archiwum Akt Nowych. He gave me access

16. Macek Roszkowski aboard the *Hoorn*. Like Scratch in Washington DC, Macek and his wife, Basia, let me stay at their place when I did research in Warsaw. Courtesy of the author.

to some communist party documents and trade ministry records. I was, after all, revising the notion that the communist governments in the Soviet bloc were unwilling to cooperate with the West. On several occasions my document requests were denied, but I was able to get my research done. That side of my sojourn in Poland was uneventful.

My visits to Warsaw and the basketball games provided a welcome respite from the research routine. Lublin fans were excited about our first home game; the six-hundred-seat gym was packed to the gills. We won, but it was a sloppy game because the gym caretaker had put a wax shine on the floor that had us slipping and sliding. At any stop in play I ran over to the sideline to get some moisture on my soles.

Few of the opponents' gyms had over five hundred seats, but most of them were sold out, in part to see the American. Opposing players didn't single me out for rough or dirty play, except for a team from Kraków. I got a little frustrated after a couple elbows to the head and turned to one player and said, "Fuck you." Most Poles didn't speak much English in those days, and I figured that my expletive would go unnoticed, but the guy responded with his own "Fuck you!" Surprised, I broke out laughing.

It is no secret that Poles like their vodka. In fact, some are embarrassed by their drinking culture, which tends to sloppy drunkenness—too akin to those barbarian Russians to the east. Many Poles were envious of the Germans and French and their more sophisticated beer and wine cultures. I witnessed quite a few street brawls between inebriated Poles.

One afternoon a couple of University of Warsaw historians invited me to a meeting to discuss my dissertation. Instead of tea or coffee, they pulled out a bottle of vodka and three glasses. I slowly sipped my straight vodka while the other two finished off the bottle. They weren't much help with my research. During a game we played in Katowice, our bus driver got so drunk at a nearby bar that he could not drive the bus back to Lublin. The team had to take the train home.

Lublin was only sixty miles from the Soviet border, but I didn't try to get a visa to go. In those days it was mandatory to have an invitation from someone, in part to prove that you had a place to stay. Even staying in a hotel without notice was problematic. When the team stayed overnight on road games, they never registered me. I stayed out of view of the front desk until they had procured the rooms. On a road trip to Rzeszów in southeast Poland, the team asked the bus driver to take me to the Soviet border, which was only about twenty miles away. One teammate turned to me and growled in a derisive, angry tone as if to rue the cruel geographical fate of the Polish people: "There it is. The Soviet Union."

Shortly before I left Poland I told a reporter from *Rzeczpospolita* that I had been asked to throw a game. In European leagues the bottom two or three teams drop out of their division into the next lower one—a process called relegation—and the top teams from the lower division move up. Toward the end of the season teams threatened with relegation might approach a team in the middle of the standings to shave points. Start Lublin, our city rival, was in that precarious rele-

17. The AZS Lublin basketball team before my last game. I am third from the right, proudly wearing the Polish national basketball warmup suit that the team gave me that day. Piotr "Big Red" Karolak, the best player on the team, is second from the left. The AZS Polish eagle banners behind us are sans the crown, which I put back on for the team T-shirts as a subtle jab at the communist regime. Courtesy of the author.

gation position, and tried to get me to sandbag. I was shocked and immediately declined. The offer got into my head, however, because if I didn't play well people would *think* that I had thrown the game. I stunk up the place and we lost that game.

AZS Lublin finished fourth in the second league, the highest finish in club history. The last shot I took with Lublin was a three-pointer to secure the win against Siarka Tarnobrzeg. I yelled to Piotr Karolak, our best young player, "Za trzy!" (For three!)—a little inside joke that we had used all season on big three-pointers. What a sweet way to finish the year.

I even won over the communist press. *Sztandar Ludu* (People's Banner), the local party organ, published a big article, "Farewell to Anderson," reporting the celebration at the end of the game was "spontaneous and touching . . . with flowers, crystal bowls, and mementos from the team." Most of the best Polish products were exported to the West for hard currency, but a couple of valuable things Poles could buy were silver and amber jewelry as well as crystal. I didn't have room in my luggage for the big, heavy crystal bowls, so I had to leave them with our coach. The team also gave me a red and white warm-up jacket with "Polska" emblazoned on the back, which I proudly wore for years until it fell apart.

The newspaper noted that AZS Lublin, made up mostly of young student-athletes, had "reason to be satisfied" with "good prospects for the future," adding that "the young players can't forget about Sheldon Anderson's important role in their success. The likable American brought a lot of new elements to the gym. Thank you, Sheld!"

In fact the team gave me greater memories than I gave them. I told *Kurier Lubelski*, "I learned a lot in my stay in your country. And I think that I imparted the AZS players some valuable skills. It was great to make so many friends. I'd like to come back in a year." I was not referring to playing again but to visiting all of the close friends I had made in Poland. Later that summer Baran told the paper that "Anderson wants to come back to [play for] Lublin." I had told Baran that if the team needed me for a big game I might be able to fly back. But at thirty-eight it was time to finish the PhD and find a real job. I had my research in the bag, thanks to Baran, AZS Lublin, and the Roszkowskis.

8

The Shot Doctor of Philosophy

I received my PhD in the fall of 1989 and was on a one-year teaching job at the University of Puget Sound in Tacoma when I heard the astonishing news that the Berlin Wall had come down. The Cold War was over. The fall of the Wall was the last act of World War II. After four decades of Soviet-backed communist rule, my friends in Poland and East Germany were finally free.

November 9 cannot be celebrated as a German holiday, however; that date is also associated with the horrors of Kristallnacht—the Night of Broken Glass—when in 1938 Hitler unleashed his henchmen in a rampage on Jewish homes and businesses. It was a portent to the Holocaust.

I teach a class called "World History since 1945," in which I tell my students that, despite all of the relentlessly bad news that they get through their ubiquitous media platforms, the world is in a lot better place today than it was at the end of World War II. All of the European empires fell apart in the decades after the war. Ask Africans and Asians if they would like to be ruled again from London, Paris, Brussels, or Lisbon. My folks used to say to me at mealtime, "Clean your plate, Sheldon. There are starving people in China." That didn't mean anything to me except to count my blessings, but in fact there *were* starving people in China—some thirty million of them. Ask the Chinese if they want to go back to those days of Mao's mad Great Leap Forward. It is remarkable how much progress that country has made in the last several decades. And who can argue that since 1945 women and oppressed minorities have not made great strides toward basic equality and human rights? Ask them if they want to return to the kitchen and Jim Crow.

In 1989 Eastern Europe freed itself from communist dictatorship; two years later the Soviet Union fell apart. Although the specter of authoritarian rule is still real there, ask the people if they want to return to Stalinism.

As the crisis in the GDR unfolded that fall, the Hentzes, my friends from Halle, hungrily watched West German television to get the news. The East German media was spewing its usual falsehoods about the reactionary demonstrations on the streets of Berlin, Leipzig, and Dresden, emphasizing instead the fortieth anniversary of the founding of the GDR.

East Germans were finally emboldened to stand up against the regime. When hundreds of thousands joined the demonstrations, Erich Mielke, the head of East German security, told the communist party chief, Erich Honecker, "We can't beat them all up." Lori Hentze recalled the first time she actually "voted" in a GDR election, by crossing out *all* of the names on the communist party list. There were no other alternatives on the ballot. The election officials, all party members, took note of this silent protest, but by that time the GDR was in its death throes.

Lori and Harald Hentze decided not to join the wave of East Germans leaving through the open Hungarian-Austrian border. Where to go? Where to work? Both had good jobs and two daughters in school, and Halle was their home. They thought that the GDR regime might change, but never imagined that the state would wither away and Germany would reunify. Many East Germans who impulsively left the GDR in 1989 found no work or future in West Germany and returned to their old homes.

In the last few years of the GDR it was possible to get a visa to visit close West German relatives. In early 1989 Harald applied for a visa to visit an aunt in Hamburg. Because he was a teacher, his case was immediately reported to the police. The Stasi had already asked a neighbor to spy on the Hentzes, but he declined. Surprisingly Harald got the visa and left for West Germany in May. On the way he stopped in Köln (Cologne) to see the magnificent Gothic cathedral, which Lori had said was for her a symbol of divided Germany, and the feeling that she would never get there to see it.

When the Wall fell that November, Harald immediately got in his Trabant again to see friends in Erlangen, near Frankfurt. He brought roses from the Hentze garden, some of which he gave to the East German guards and the rest to his friends. Those "German roses" were pressed, framed, and hung in a special place—a poignant reminder of that beautiful moment.

Lori made preparations to visit her French friend Martine, who had visited Halle every four years before the Wall fell. Lori had not been allowed to go the other way; she had applied for a visa in the fall of 1988 but was denied. As Martine's family was leaving from their last trip to the GDR in the summer of 1988, her young son had asked how long four years was. Lori broke down in tears.

With the Iron Curtain opened, now Lori would visit France. In late November the Hentze family drove to Erlangen to visit Harald's friends and to pick up their one hundred D-Mark *Begrüssungsgeld*, a one-time gift that the West German government gave to first-time East German visitors. Unsurprisingly, Lori said it was an "insane feeling" to cross the border, probably akin to a prisoner getting a pardon from a lifetime sentence. A month later the family was on a train to France. Martine and her family met them in Metz. Tears gushed. When they got to Paris and were walking down the Champs-Élysées, Lori kept poking Harald just to assure herself that this was not a dream. It was a blessing for her mother to know that her daughter had made it to the West.

Harald, like many of his compatriots, became a capitalist overnight. For the next several months he drove to Berlin on the weekends to chink off concrete pieces of the Wall to sell to western tourists. Harald found a piece of the wall that, oddly enough, had my name in black magic marker and a spray-painted red, white, and blue background. He made about $7,000 for around forty days of work; some East Germans who worked at the Wall seven days a week made nearly six figures. So much for the notion that East Germans had become committed Marxists.

Successful revolutions are always hardest on the middle-aged. The collapse of the East German state in 1990 hit Lori's brother, Walter Detzer, and his wife hard; they struggled to adapt to life in the new, unified German state. Walter taught electronics, but he would have to return to school for a refresher course on more advanced western technology. Although West German authorities kept many East German teachers in their jobs, they were paid less than their West German counterparts. Heidi lost her job with Mitropa and could not find meaningful new work. Crime in East Berlin increased after the fall of the Wall; they were worried about their future in this wild and woolly capitalist world.

Heidi sought solace in the company of other disgruntled "Ossis"—short for *Ostdeutsche* (East Germans). If she met them on vacation, she would commiserate about West Germany's misdeeds in dismantling the positive elements of the East German system, such as the generous social system and total employment. *Anschluss*, or annexation, is the German word used to describe Hitler's take-over of Austria in March 1938, but some Ossis co-opted it to describe West Germany's incorporation of East Germany into the Federal Republic in 1990. About one in three Germans living in the former GDR today think that unification was a failure.

They had some reason to complain. Three decades after German unification, unemployment in the former East German states is still much higher than in the West German side. Heidi and many of her East German compatriots blamed "capitalists" from the West for buying up East German assets and then shutting most of them down. Heidi imagined that East German enterprises, if given a chance, could have become profitable and competitive. She said East Germans had been brainwashed into thinking that all western goods were superior; in her view, they had accelerated the collapse of East German industry by refusing to buy the old "socialist" products. In fact, other than some small shops like bakeries, few East German companies could have competed.

A month after the fall of the Berlin Wall, I flew from Seattle to Cincinnati to interview for a tenure-track job at Miami University. After arriving in Oxford late the night before, the chair of the Miami history department took me to breakfast at 7 a.m., which was 4 a.m. Pacific time. Bleary-eyed, I barely touched the eggs and bacon as I tried to make an impression on my would-be boss. A battery of interviews with deans and faculty followed; late in the afternoon I gave the department a lecture on my dissertation. Those "job talks" can make or break you, and I was exhausted.

My lecture was on Poland's contribution to the Marshall Plan. When I was in graduate school, many leftist U.S. foreign policy historians were blaming the United States as much as Stalin for the division of Europe after World War II. The Marshall Plan, NATO, and the rearmament of West Germany were seen as capitalist efforts to keep socialism out of Western Europe; these efforts, it was charged, antagonized the Kremlin enough that Stalin decided to impose communist dictatorships in every East European state.

Staunch Cold Warriors would have none of this view, especially East European émigrés. To them Stalin was as bad as Hitler, and his communist lackeys in Eastern Europe were morally bankrupt. Some American scholars vilified a colleague of mine at Miami for arguing that the numbers of people Stalin killed in the purges were inflated. He contended that many Soviets supported Stalin's regime, and that the totalitarian image of the Soviet state was false. Right-wingers wanted to cast the Soviet dictator as more evil than Hitler, and therefore equally dangerous to the West. In 1996 one critic wrote of my friend's work that "it is absurd to write airily of 'popular support' in a system where no free political choices were possible and where the population was subject to an endless drubbing by state-monopolized propaganda." My colleague recalled that he "was tormented at the time." In fact, he made an important corrective to the totalitarian image of the Soviet state.

My dissertation fell somewhere in between these schools of thought. There is no doubt that Stalin was responsible for the Iron Curtain and that he wanted to secure his western border from another attack. After all, Germany had invaded Russia twice in the first half of the twentieth century. Spreading communism into Western Europe was a secondary goal.

Stalin did not envision the complete isolation of his sphere of influence from the West, especially economically. Although the Polish election of January 1947 was clearly rigged in favor of the communists, the Stalinist government continued to trade with the West, and Polish coal was essential to Western European economic recovery.

Leftists liked the premise of my work, which eventually became my first book. At the job talk at Miami, another professor in the history department—a noted scholar of Nixon and the Vietnam War—wanted me to affirm that U.S. policies had been responsible for the division of Europe. I was not willing to say that but I got the job anyway. Despite our minor theoretical differences, that professor and his wife became my best friends in town.

A couple of years later I was invited to a seminar in Washington DC headed by Gar Alperowitz, who was a major figure in this leftist critique of U.S. foreign policy. He made it his life's work to prove that President Harry Truman did not drop the atomic bombs on Japan to end the war, but to intimidate Stalin into making political concessions in postwar Europe and keep the Soviet Union out of Japan. One of his main arguments was that the bombs were unnecessary

18. My best friends in the Miami University History Department, ca. 1996. "Ice" is on the far right, Jeff Kimball next to him, and his wife, Linda Musmeci, is holding my son, O Max. My wife, Kristie, is in the middle. Courtesy of the author.

because Japan was in negotiations with the Soviet Union about a possible end to the war.

Of course the Japanese leaders were seeking a *conditional* surrender because Japanese cities were getting bombed to bits and their military situation was hopeless. The Allies had embarked on bombing civilians long before the bombs were dropped in August 1945. More lives were lost in the fire bombings of Tokyo than perished at Hiroshima. Given the Japanese code of military honor, the Americans doubted that the Japanese would ever agree to an unconditional surrender. Truman didn't lose any sleep over using the atomic bomb to end the war. My uncle was one of those GIS headed to the Far East for the final invasion of Japan; the bomb may have saved his life. Ironically, it also spared Japan of more casualties if the United States had invaded the home islands. That Truman and his advisers also saw political advantage in using the bomb to intimidate Stalin is obvious, but that was *not* Truman's main goal.

The academics at the Alperowitz seminar also wanted me to confirm that Washington was to blame for the Cold War. My nuanced response was not warmly received. Likewise, historians of Polish foreign policy, especially those of Polish heritage, were not interested in giving the Polish communist government any credit for cooperating with the West, even economically. Wojciech Roszkowski, my contact to get into the Warsaw archives, dismissed my attempts to talk about the moderates and realists in the Polish communist government. He called them all a bunch of prostitutes.

This was early in my academic career, and I took those critiques hard. I still had that nagging feeling that I was not a bona fide scholar. In 2000 I was invited to a conference on Ronald Reagan, where I gave a paper on Reagan's role in the fall of communism. Most Americans credit Reagan's hard-line policies in forcing Soviet premier Mikhail Gorbachev to end the Cold War and allowing the Soviet satellites to go their own way, but I argued that Gorbachev was the key player in 1989. He knew that the communist system was falling farther and farther behind the West, and that it was inhumane to boot. I had seen that for myself in East Germany and Poland. Gorbachev wanted to reduce exorbitant military spending and to make market economic reforms. He did not foresee that the entire edifice would come crumbling down.

To Reagan's credit, in his second term in office he softened his policies toward the Soviet Union and developed a warm relationship with Gorbachev. It was not Reagan the tough guy who ended the Cold War, but Reagan the compromiser. When the *New York Times* quoted what I had said at the conference, I felt that I might finally have made the transition from jock to scholar.

Nonetheless basketball continued to play an important part in my life. I was lucky to be still playing "the child's game," as Celtic great Bill Russell called it. I thought it was cool when, during one Augsburg summer league game, former Gopher and NBA Hall of Famer Kevin McHale blocked what I thought was a sure layup. I'll take it from a guy who made the 1997 list of the top fifty NBA players of all time. In 1989 I played hooky from a history conference in Cincinnati to find a game at the local downtown YMCA. Who was playing but none other than another legend on that list—"The Big O"—Oscar Robertson, the biggest name ever to play in that town. What an honor to get scored on by him, but he got a little ornery when his team lost. So do I when I lose.

In the mid-1980s, I teamed up with Fitz, my old high school teammate Keith Hardeman, and Brad Olson, my co-captain at Augsburg, to form an AAU team in Minneapolis, reprising what was the norm before World War II—barnstorming teams that traveled from small town to small town playing baseball or basketball games. Along with the Pillsbury Kings, we were the best post-college team in Minnesota, beating guys from the University of Minnesota and other D-I schools. We had two D-I centers, Roger Anderson, who backed up John Shumate at Notre Dame, and Gopher Tom Masterson. We used to call Roger, Tom, and Keith our aircraft carriers. The rest of us got all of the shots and accolades, but we would have gone nowhere without those guys defending, rebounding, passing, and picking.

We drove all over Minnesota and Wisconsin to get games, most of them in the dead of winter. On one road trip to Eau Claire, Wisconsin, we drove back to Minneapolis in a serious blizzard. We got on I-94 right before the cops began closing the interstate behind us. I led the other two team cars in my aging Olds station wagon. Eventually we had about ten cars in our caravan, all following my taillights as I drove about ten miles an hour down the road. We passed dozens of cars in the ditch along the way. I couldn't see past the front of the car, so Keith, sitting shotgun, told me how close I was getting to the reflecting poles on the shoulder. At one point we mistakenly followed the reflectors off an exit ramp; all of the cars behind me, including the complete strangers, followed as we went off the freeway and then back on it. The ninety-mile trip took four hours. While I was white-knuckling it, Masterson, sitting in the back of the car, was pounding brewskies.

I might be most proud of the championships I won in the summer of 1987, when I was thirty-six, and another nearly ten years later. In the mid-1980s the NBA started a pro-am league in St. Paul. I played with a couple of big aircraft carriers again—Steve Lingenfelter, who played two years in the NBA with the Washington Bullets and the San Antonio Spurs, and Chris Engler, who played six years in the NBA with five different teams. Engler was the king of the NBA ten-day contracts, parlaying them into an NBA pension when he retired. It was fun but aggravating to play with those guys. Lingenfelter got fouled a lot but couldn't shoot a lick from the foul line, and hot-headed Engler got at least one technical a game.

The high scorer on our championship team was University of Detroit alum Greg Wendt. He was the 139th pick of the 1986 NBA draft but didn't make the Boston Celtics roster. A 6'6" lefty, Greg was deadly from mid-range. Defense was optional. Both Greg and his wife, Kathy, had lucrative jobs in Minneapolis at the time, but when he found out that I had played ball in Germany, he asked me about hooking him up with a team. I put him in touch with Bramsche, a team near Osnabrück in the second division. Much to my surprise, Greg and Kathy pulled up stakes and went to Europe, where Greg played for five years. To his credit, Herr Wendt, as I call him, learned the language and assimilated into the culture of his forebears.

In the late 1980s a couple of brothers began the "Gus Macker 3-on-3 Basketball Tournament," an outdoor road show that brought portable baskets to cities around the Midwest. In 1996 the tournament came to the streets of St. Paul. I enlisted Chris Elzey, who had played at Penn and is now a history professor at George Mason University, and Billy McKee, an old rival from St. Thomas who played on our AAU team.

Chris is the best shooter I have ever seen; HORSE games with him are marathons. Whenever we get together in any setting, we play. I hold the Rustic HORSE Championship (played on dirt at my lake cabin), but I think he owns the Outdoor, Indoor, and Canadian titles. He came to Minnesota for a year in 1996 and landed an assistant coaching job with the St. Paul Slam, a fledgling (now defunct) minor league basketball team. Chris would have been the best player on the team. The head coach always asked him to play, but Chris told me he didn't want to play with a team that had little basketball IQ. The coach didn't have much either; whenever he played with Chris in a pickup game the coach always took more shots. With a money shooter like Chris, pass the ball!

The winter of 1996–97 was one of the worst in recent Minnesota history. The Slam had road trips to the far reaches of North and South Dakota, where the team was often caught in blizzards. During one particularly bad snowstorm, a player on the team turned to Chris and observed, "This is like Napoleon and shit." Maybe the guy didn't have much court sense, but at least he knew about the Little Corporal's fateful foray into the Russian winter in 1812.

Billy was a great defensive player, but in my senior year against St. Thomas I scored thirty-nine points, twenty on Billy in the first half. His buddy Paige Piper guarded me in the second half and always kidded Billy that he had held me to nineteen. By the time we played the Macker, Billy was a better player than I was.

Chris was thirty, Billy forty-four, and I was forty-five. We were all under 6'3", but we were the best shooters in the top division of the tournament. The Macker rules give you one point for a shot inside the "three-point" arc and two points for a shot outside it. When other teams, including a lot of young D-I players, saw their aging opponents, they thought they had a cake walk. As we barreled through our bracket the growing crowd in downtown St. Paul began to cheer for the old guys who played the game the right way, as my Carolina Cougars' tryout coach Larry Brown used to say, and, given the rules, the smart way. I had a wide open layup in

19. A *Stammtisch* in Oxford with some of my favorite basketballers from the Miami University rec center. They have kept me young at heart, if not in body. Courtesy of the author.

one game when I dished it out to Chris at the arc. Someone in the crowd yelled, "What are you doing?" After the pass I turned to him and said, "Watch." Bang! Chris hit the shot for two points instead of one. The crowd chuckled. It was a most satisfying tournament win in a stupid street ball game.

I still play with the students at the Miami rec center, where I get to know the men and women who would rarely show up in my diplomatic history courses. I call it my unofficial hard-court office hours. I'm still all too competitive, but when I don't care about winning I will quit. I always kid the students that if they don't pass me the ball, or play the right way, they'd better not show up in one of my courses. I admitted to the Miami student newspaper that "I'm often not the nicest guy on the court, so if I see a student later with whom I had played, I'll say, 'I was a real jerk, wasn't I?'"

I had one more stint at playing basketball for compensation. In 1993 I taught at Miami's branch campus in Luxembourg City, so I searched out a team in Trier, Germany, just across the Luxembourg border. A fourth league team offered me the free use of a car for the season. What fun it was to play competitive games again, and even to practice with the team. The European club sports system enables athletes to play in well-organized leagues well into their later years. Most American players have finished their high school and college careers in their early twenties, and are relegated to playing in pickup games.

This peculiar link between educational institutions and sports has a long history in the United States. At the D-I college level it has led to repeated rules violations. It is a system geared to preparing players for a professional sports career rather than an honest dedication to academics. Coaches have to win to keep their jobs; even at the mid-major level they can make more than the college president. Keeping players eligible is the bottom line.

Indiana University basketball coach Bobby Knight was the poster boy for what was and is wrong with college sports. Although Knight supposedly ran a "clean" program and graduated most of his players, he was a belligerent bully. Like me, Knight was a public university employee, but he could throw temper tantrums on the court, toss chairs, and belittle, berate, and even choke his student-athletes. If I tried that in the classroom I'd be out of a job in a heartbeat. In 2000 when Knight grabbed a student by the arm for yelling to him, "Hey Knight, what's up?" the Indiana administration finally fired him. Many Hoosier students and fans rioted in protest.

Years later, I happened to see Knight in the Minneapolis airport. I almost yelled at him, "Hey Knight," but I chickened out. I didn't want to be the second guy in Minneapolis to get punched out by a sports celebrity. In 1979 New York Yankees manager Billy Martin had famously clocked a marshmallow salesman during a barroom brawl, or so the story goes.

In the first session of my sports history course I get into one of the student's faces à la Knight and angrily yell, "You better take this course seriously! If you don't I'll be right down your throat again!" The student shrinks back and the class is stunned. Then I show them photos of the irate faces of D-I coaches, including Knight, and say, "If my fellow university employees can behave this way toward students, why can't I?" They realize that I am joking, but they get the point.

It is no secret that the NCAA is running a corrupt for-profit system under the guise of amateurism. The NCAA makes hundreds of millions of dollars on D-I men's football and basketball, and top coaches in those sports make millions while most athletes get a tuition voucher and a spoon-fed, easy course of study.

How many academic scandals, illegal under-the-table payments to players, one-and-done basketball players, scalawag multimillionaire coaches like John Calipari will it take before college presidents honestly evaluate the value of D-I sports to the academic mission of their universities? The University of Chicago got rid of football in 1939, and that worked out pretty well for that top-notch school (it has D-III football now).

The best solution might be to divorce teams from the university budget and make them self-sufficient, self-funding clubs that pay the players. Players could choose to use their money to go to school. Alabama or UCLA could still lay claim to their football or basketball "clubs" without having to do a phony dance to keep their "student"-athletes NCAA-eligible. After all, Alabama football is a religion, and the game is the weekly mass. Nike, Walmart, or Amazon would love to put their stamp on D-I teams. Players do not even have the right to sell their likeness, although in 2019 California passed a law to allow it. That could signal the end of the entire NCAA system of "amateur" athletics.

Years ago when the D-I players at Miami were not allowed to practice with their coaches in the off season, the varsity came over to the rec center to play with the other students. One was Wally Szczerbiak, whose father, Walt, was a standout player for Real Madrid at the same time I was playing in Germany. Walt used to play one-on-one with my friend Dave Smith, who was a diplomat in the U.S. Embassy in Madrid. I had played against Dave many times in college and we had become best friends after. Wally had an outstanding NCAA tournament in his senior year, and coincidentally was drafted by the Minnesota Timberwolves. I took my son, Max, to see a game once, and brought him down to the bench to meet Wally.

My other favorite Miami player was Devon Davis, who with his outrageously cool dreadlock updo led Miami to the Mid-American Conference Tournament Championship and an NCAA tournament berth in 1995. Davis liked having me on his team because I always passed him the ball; if it came back to me, I could nail the three-pointer.

I don't see the Miami varsity in the gym much anymore. D-I athletes have become more and more isolated from the student body. They can work out with coaches year round and have their own separate training facilities and training tables. Academic advisers steer them into courses and independent studies that they are sure to pass. Coaches have to feign commitment to the importance of a college education. One Miami football player told me recently that when he was recruited, a Miami assistant coach held up two fingers and told him, "Academics come first." Holding up one finger the coach said, "Football comes second."

It is not the coaches' fault that they have to put winning first and cut corners to keep their players eligible, regardless of the detriment to the "student" side of the student-athlete. Losing coaches don't keep their jobs, regardless of their players' high graduation rates. A few years ago I noticed several huge guys walking into a classroom across from my office. Obviously they were football players. It was a western civilization course taught by an elderly history faculty member; evidently the athletic department knew that by that time he was just phoning it in and giving easy grades. A year later I taught the same course, but I didn't have one football player. I rarely have male athletes in my sports history course either, probably because the reading load is heavy and I only give essay exams. Even at a top academic school like Miami, advisers steer players into easy majors and courses.

In 1993 the head coach of the men's basketball team, Joby Wright, left to coach at the University of Wyoming. I applied for the Miami coaching job, knowing that I wouldn't get it, but I thought my application might make the search committee think about the priorities of athletics at the D-I level. I began my letter to the search committee, "Admittedly it is unusual for a Miami faculty member to apply for a coaching position, but given the wide gap that has developed between the mission of Miami's D-I athletic programs and the educational mission of the university, now may be a good time to hire a coach who is dedicated to education first and to winning basketball games second." I went on to list my college and professional basketball credentials, as well as my success as a teacher, which, after all, is what makes a good coach. I love to mentor kids and I know the game. Although I was right there on campus, the search committee did not even give me the courtesy of a rejection letter. They could have sent it through campus mail, saving the cost of a postage stamp.

I did have the chance to coach my kids' basketball, baseball, softball, and soccer teams, which was more gratifying anyway. Max and Lauren played out of John J. Pershing Park in south Minneapolis, so naturally I named the various iterations of their baseball teams the "Generals," the "Black Jacks," the "Doughboys," and the "E Force." I had their T-shirts made with interlocking bats of two hitters, who are wearing not caps but rather the flat helmets of U.S. soldiers in the Great War. I still have those one-of-a-kind shirts as a reminder of those precious father-son, father-daughter times.

Even though they were just kids' games—and I never ever yelled at the umps, the other players and coaches, or my minions—I wanted to win. Why play sports if you don't keep score? My players always wanted to win, too. Some bleeding-heart liberals want to make sure that no kid feels bad when they lose, but those are the important lessons that sport teaches. Not everyone can win; taking a loss hard but learning to accept it graciously is a good life lesson. Life comes with hard knocks.

Max's friends have grown up now. I love to tell them stories about their high and low moments. They get more laughs about their big mental boo-boos, which were in fact more often mistakes on my part. In one game when they were about eleven, we were ahead by one in the last inning, with Erik on the mound. The other team got the bases loaded with one out, so I went to the mound, pulled an outfielder into the infield and told all five infielders that we were going to go home with the ball for a force-out to cut off the tying run. Erik winds up, and the batter hits a grounder back to him. "Yes!" It's an easy force-out at home. But "No!" Erik turns to throw the ball to first, allowing the tying run to score. Worse, he throws the ball over the first baseman's head, and the kid from second trots home with the winning run. I own that one. I had expressly told the infielders to throw home, assuming that Erik had heard me, too, and that he would pick up on the fact that I had brought in an extra infielder and that the infield was playing in to throw home. Nope. It is always remarkable to me how many Major Leaguers make the same kinds of mistakes.

Max and his buddies were losing a basketball game by two with ten seconds left when Max got fouled. He went to the line and coolly hit both to tie the game. Somehow he thought we were still down one; on the inbounds pass he intentionally fouled, putting the opposing player on the line for the winning free throw. I had informed the other players not to foul after Max (hopefully) had tied the game, but I didn't say anything to him, wanting to make sure that he concentrated on making the shots. My bad, as the kids say. After his second free throw I should have substituted a player who had had the no-foul instructions.

One of my favorite baseball players was Max's friend Morgan, a very bright but impish kid who didn't quite have a knack for the game. Time after time he missed my signs to steal a base. Finally I just ran my index and middle fingers over my forearm like someone running. He got that one. After we got back to the bench I reminded him of the steal sign. "Have you got it? Hat and then sleeve means steal." So Morgan gets on first and I run my hand over my hat and sleeve for him to steal. Then I did a couple of other phony signs so the other team wouldn't decipher the real one. The pitcher fired the ball and Morgan just stood there. After the inning was over I asked him if he had seen the steal sign. "Yes," he replied. "But I got confused by the other signs you gave." Aaargh.

I admit that I have a love affair with sports, which will come as no surprise to my wife. In 2019 a California judge ruled that the NCAA was running an illegal cartel, but did nothing to break it up because there was no alternative to the system. The judge knew that sports fans love the college game. I am guilty. In spite of my misgivings about the system, I hold my nose and watch D-I college basketball and football. For a die-hard sports fan, what is more fun than the men's NCAA basketball tournament? I just wish it was on the up and up.

For over fifteen years my brother, Randy, and Dave Smith went to the Mirage hotel in Las Vegas to wager on the first round of March Madness. I joined them after several years. Until the late 2010s Nevada was the only state to allow sports betting. Vegas mogul Steve Wynn loved to bet on sports, so when he built the Mirage in the late 1980s he included the biggest sports book in town, with three huge TV screens.

About 120 inveterate gamblers filled the seats at the Mirage for the first March Madness weekend. Some of us did shifts through the night to hang on to those precious seats to watch four straight days of basketball. No one wants to stand all day. We bet on any and every basketball game, including the NBA and the National Invitation Tournament.

Gamblers have always bet on sports, but in the old days no bookie would take a bet on a heavy favorite. The spread is the points that are given to the underdog in a game, theoretically making it a fifty-fifty chance to win. The spread had its roots in what bookies in the 1940s called the Minneapolis Clearinghouse, run by firm president Leo Hirschfield. Bookies used the Clearinghouse lines in illegal gambling, but as Hirschfield said, tongue-in-cheek, "If a man buys the line, it's not my business what he does with it. If I were to sell you a car, do you think I'd ask if you planned to rob a bank?" The point spread was a brilliant idea, because gamblers could bet on *either* team, and the bookie had more action.

We used to bet on the NCAA women's basketball tournament, but Vegas stopped hanging lines on the women's tournament because the casinos were losing money. The oddsmakers didn't do enough homework on those games, and the wiseguys took advantage. We had one guy in our group who researched the women's teams for us; those were our most lucrative wagers. We'd bet on the UConn women to cover a fifty-point spread—they usually did.

Every year we saw the same people at the Mirage: Danny and his Colorado Boys, the Cincinnati Crew, and, our favorites, the New Jersey Guys, who had met at Syracuse University. They always bet on their beloved Orange and coach Jim Boeheim—"The Thin Man," as we called him. The Jersey Guys' ringleader was Mike "The Middler" Gross, who got his nickname for his pet bet, a complicated half-time wager called "playing the middle." If your initial bet on the game looks like an easy winner, you place a second-half spread wager on the *other* team. I used to rib him, "So, Middler, you have this bet locked up—you picked the right side for the game—but now you are going to lose it by 'playing the middle.'"

The Middler and his buddy Gary Applebaum, a.k.a. "The Bomb," bet a lot of long-shot money lines, a wager on the underdog without getting the spread points. As anyone who has been in a sports book knows, gamblers love to strut their big wins but rarely reveal their losses. "Who do you like?" is the most oft-asked question at a sports book. Bettors are always trying to get an angle—the can't-lose tip on a "lock bet." The sports books should have a "lock-bet line" in front of a teller handing out Kleenexes to the miserable losers.

Randy made our group the talk of the Mirage sports book. We were known as the "Hat Guys," and Randy was the "Hat Daddy." He bought hats of every team in the tournament (sixty-eight teams), and duplicates of teams like Duke and Michigan State that were in the tournament every year. In the morning Randy would bring down a bag full of hats to the book. Before the games went off he would ask people sitting around us what team they had bet on and give them a hat to wear for good luck. After the game Hat Daddy collected his hats, put them back into his bag and readied the next batch. Sometimes a disgruntled loser (never our good friends) would hurl the hat back at Randy. That ingrate never got another one to wear. Get in the lock-bet line.

Hat Daddy had expensive bowling shirts made emblazoned with our monikers; I was "The Professor," Dave Smith was "Stat Man" (he brought huge binders full of statistics to beat the book), and Kevin Meyer, who had played football for Barry Switzer at Oklahoma, was "The Cooler." Old Vegas really believed in people who were inherently star-crossed, hiring them to stand next to a player on a winning streak. William H. Macy portrayed a cooler in the movie of the same name, but when he finds love he loses his unlucky touch. Our cooler had an indefatigably defeatist attitude, sinking deeper and deeper into his chair as bet after bet went south. He never let on if he was winning. Regardless, The Cooler was always good for a dozen Krispy Kremes, to start our long days on a healthy note.

Big Lou Conte was the Jersey Guys' version of The Cooler, but he always kept a happy-go-lucky mien. He loved the Hat Guys' high jinks, like when for shits and giggles we bet what we dubbed the "full monte"—five different bets on the same team. Big Lou was always digging into Hat Daddy's bag of furry college team mascots, matching them up to determine his bet.

Randy maintained that the Mirage should have comped us rooms, food, and drink, because the Hat Guys and Jersey Guys brought publicity to the hotel, as well as fun to the whole room (of course the casino doesn't care about fun unless it translates into profit). We weren't "whales"—the big gamblers that the casinos cater to—but the tellers at the Mirage got a kick out of our personalized bowling shirts, the mascots, and the goofy novelty hats, like the big red chili pepper I wore when the Ragin' Cajuns of Louisiana were playing or the buffalo head for the North Dakota State Bison.

We also put the Mirage in the national news. In 2005 the *Washington Post* ran a story on sports betting at the Mirage, headlined "March Madness Turns Gamblers into Basket Cases." The Hat Guys were central to the story. "The Hat Man unzips his thick duffle bag and whips out a burgundy Eastern Kentucky hat and a Kentucky blue one," the reporter wrote, "which he hands to his brother, Sheldon, 53, a European history scholar at Miami (Ohio). . . . For nine years they've worn whatever hat their money's on for luck." The piece also featured Big Lou: "Day One hasn't been kind to Conte either. Having given up on his first strategy (smarts), he's going with Plan B: picking games according to which mascot would win a hypothetical battle. Bobcat vs. Gator is no easy pick, mind you [Ohio University vs Florida Gators]. Would the Gator drown the Bobcat? Or would the Bobcat slit the Gator's throat first? Suddenly Conte looks up and beams. 'Lock of the day!' he bellows. 'Cyclone against a Gopher!' [Iowa State to beat Minnesota]."

In 2013 the Hat Guys even turned up on National Public Radio (NPR). Someone at the sports book told Ted Robbins to talk to us. When he sat down next to me, Robbins knew he had an angle: "The Hat Guys and the Jersey Guys are in big comfy seats and they're here for the duration. Sheldon Anderson and his brother Randy are the hat guys. They have a bag full of caps from every team they bet on. The Jersey Guys are not wearing jerseys, they're from New Jersey.

Michael Gross started this tradition 19 years ago. 'I am the culprit,' Mike admitted. 'We met them [the Hat Guys] here. We don't know them, but now we're fast friends. And we hug and kiss and we love each other for five days. We go nuts. . . . [It's] the best week of the year.'" Robbins concluded, "This is what they have in common. . . . They are kindred spirits in March Madness."

Some of my colleagues at Miami heard that NPR broadcast and thought it was hilarious. But I found out through the grapevine that the chair of the history department was not happy, thinking that I was AWOL in Vegas. I was livid that she had not come to me first about allegedly shirking my teaching duties, and I confronted her about it. She sheepishly retreated when I told her that I had never canceled a class in all of the years I had been going to Vegas. As much as I love to play and watch sports, my students' academic achievement has always taken priority. I wish the NCAA would feel the same.

Epilogue

Ironically the last stop on my basketball odyssey is St. Paul, that strange place across the Mississippi from my hometown. Dennis Fitzpatrick, my old nemesis from St. Thomas College, and other local basketball junkies have been running a pickup game there for over forty years. Many of our old friends have passed on.

Fitz is known as The Godfather of "Noon Ball" because as a freelance sports equipment salesman he always has time for the midday run. I call him "Fly," a nickname Fitz gave himself after the legendary high scorer from Austin Peay State University, James "Fly" Williams, a guy who really *could* jump. He evoked the cheeky cheer, "The Fly is open—let's go Peay!"

Basketball has been an important part of my life, but it is Fitz's raison d'être. He knows so many prominent people in college and pro basketball that two venerable sports columnists in the Twin Cities, Charley Walters of the *St. Paul Pioneer Press* and Pat Reusse of the *Minneapolis Star Tribune*, regularly call up Fitz for some inside dope. Fitz always manages to sneak in something about Noon Ball.

Walters often chronicled the late college coach Rick Majerus's visits to St. Paul, a city Majerus loved because the neighborhood feel reminded him of his native Milwaukee. Walters described Majerus's dinners with Fitz at Cosetta's for pasta, Mancini's for steak, or Tavern on Grand for walleye. Some chichi fare at an upscale Minneapolis bistro was out of the question.

The Noon Ballers need their basketball fix. When we get booted out of one gym, Fitz always finds another. We have played in at least fifteen different gyms. There is no way this motley crew will pay big monthly fees at some pricey suburban sports club. I did play at one of those clubs (I got a discount through my wife's job) in a Saturday game that was the antithesis of Noon Ball. The younger club guys showed up in their Beemers, Mercedes, and Audis, and kept the game to themselves, excluding anyone who was not on the invited list. More than once that got them into trouble with the club management.

Former Minnesota Vikings great wide receiver Randy Moss showed up at the game with some of his buddies. After his team lost, his crew wanted to exempt him from the shootout to get into the next game. I said no, because some of our guys had the game. When Moss's guys protested, I cracked, "Who does he think he is, Randy Moss?" That didn't sit too well with him, and I got an earful. He got into the game anyway and my team beat his. Sweet justice.

Well into my sixties I was still holding my own in those highly competitive club games, but when one guy shouted at me to retire, that was it. Although I had a lot of good friends in that group, no one objected. Maybe they just thought it was trash talk. When I *really* need a run, I sneak back into that game (as a club guest). The culprit who told me to hang it up can't bring himself to apologize, but he has not objected again to my playing and even gave me a guest pass into the club one time. I know he feels bad about it.

Noon Ball is ecumenical. Anyone is allowed to play, regardless of talent or age. I used to kid one of the guys who couldn't play a lick that he was the best Armenian player I had ever seen. Little gets in the way of the game. One time fellow historian Tom Jones tore his Achilles tendon. We dragged him over to the side until Noon Ball was over. He understood.

New players get the message early on that selfish, one-on-one ball does not fly. Guys who continually miss shots elicit a curt, "There's a reason you're open." If one of the rookies persists in hogging the ball, Fitz mutters under his breath, "He doesn't get it." A couple of times Fitz brought Majerus to the game. "Full-figured but competitive as a rattlesnake," Reusse quipped. Walters joined the game once when the rotund Majerus showed up. Walters remembered, "Majerus demanded that he get to guard me—I wasn't exactly svelte either—and also demanded that my team be skins because there was no way, he said, he was going to take off his shirt. Guarding Majerus was fun because the whole time he never took a shot. Pass, pass, pass—he would always pass. He was unselfish. When a shirts teammate got selfish with the ball and took several long-range shots, Majerus, ever the coach, berated him. Loudly."

Now that my jump shot is an oxymoron, swishes surprise, and man-to-man is matador, the friendships have become a more important part of Noon Ball. We all know that paddling around in a swimming pool is our future, but there is no beauty, bonding, or fun there. Basketball is social play. Swimming is solo drudgery.

Fitz once told Walters that he would play ball "until I can't." That is a Noon Ball tradition. One of my big regrets is that injuries prematurely put old pals like Brad Olson, Keith Hardeman, and Roger Anderson on the permanent Noon Ball DL. Keith suddenly passed away sitting in his rocking chair, but Brad and Roger would probably still play if they saw the skill level of old-time ballers like Phil Webb, Fitz, and me.

I knew Phil when he played basketball at St. Paul Central with Hall of Fame baseball player Dave Winfield. Phil was an angry young Black man in those days; his hard fouls would be "Flagrant 3s" today. I recall that Fitz and I even tried to break up a fight or two between Phil and our teammates. Today Phil is one of the kindest, gentlest old souls on the court. He can't move much anymore, and because of shoulder problems he can't even shoot the ball. Phil likes to guard me because I don't call his holding and grabbing fouls, and I don't take

20. The Noon Ballers. The Godfather (Fitz) is second from the right in the second to last row. Billy McKee is in the front row, second from left. Tom Otterdahl is next to me in the second row, holding the ball. Paige Piper is in the second row second from left, and Bill Gilman is next to him. Phil Webb is far left in the last row. Courtesy of the author.

advantage of him by doubling his teammates on the offensive end (except on game point). He had a stroke recently, and his rehab at the VA Hospital was long and hard, but we told him that he was obligated to come back to Noon Ball. He did, running up and down the court a couple of times before sitting down. No matter that it was just a cameo; I hugged him and led him off the court. Phil was back.

Several Noon Ballers played with fatal illnesses. No one ever said anything about not letting them play. Bill Gilman had Lou Gehrig's disease; toward the end he couldn't lift his arms above his waist. We made gentle passes to Bill, and whomever he guarded didn't take advantage (except on game point). Larry Johns played through leukemia until he died. If there was anyone who should have dropped dead on the court it was Tom Otterdahl, who loved the game as much as Fitz. The "O-Train" still came to play after a series of small strokes. He was a chronic complainer, so even when he got sick we didn't let up on him. Fitz told Reusse about one Noon

Ball game: "Otts was in bad shape. . . . We started playing our three-man game and Otts tossed up a weak shot on a drive. Billy [McKee] goes up and just tattoos it, sends it back to midcourt. I said, 'Why did you do that, Billy?' And Billy said, 'You know as well as I do that, in two weeks, he's going to be back to being the same jerk he's always been on the court.'"

We loved the O-Train and Billy, but both are gone. In 2015 McKee succumbed to kidney cancer. He, too, played until the end. Two years later Otts died of heart failure, three days after playing his last Noon Ball game. There are only a handful of original Noon Ballers left.

I still remember the first basket that I ever made, a "granny" shot on the parsonage hoop in Moorhead. That sweet swish hooked me on a game that would take me on an improbable journey to over a dozen countries. The splash of the net has been like a rock hitting the water, sending ripples outward— small waves that have touched me and my many friends all over the world. The game itself is not a higher calling, but the people I met along the way have lifted me to a better place.